Pocket
BRUGES & BRUSSELS

TOP SIGHTS • LOCAL LIFE • MADE EASY

Helena Smith

In This Book

QuickStart Guide

Your keys to understanding the cities – we help you decide what to do and how to do it

Need to Know
Tips for a smooth trip

Neighbourhoods
What's where

Explore Bruges & Brussels

The best things to see and do, neighbourhood by neighbourhood

Top Sights
Make the most of your visit

Local Life
The insider's cities

The Best of Bruges & Brussels

The cities' highlights in handy lists to help you plan

Best Walks
See the cities on foot

Bruges & Brussels' Best...
The best experiences

Survival Guide

Tips and tricks for a seamless, hassle-free city experience

Getting Around
Travel like a local

Essential Information
Including where to stay

Our selection of the cities' best places to eat, drink and experience:

◉ **Sights**

✖ **Eating**

🍺 **Drinking**

✪ Entertainment

🔖 **Shopping**

These symbols give you the vital information for each listing:

☎ Telephone Numbers	👪 Family-Friendly
⊘ Opening Hours	🐾 Pet-Friendly
🅿 Parking	🚌 Bus
Ⓝ Nonsmoking	⛴ Ferry
@ Internet Access	Ⓜ Metro
🛜 Wi-Fi Access	Ⓢ Subway
✪ Vegetarian Selection	🚋 Tram
🗎 English-Language Menu	🚆 Train

Find each listing quickly on maps for each neighbourhood:

Bar Hemingway

16 🍺 Map p233, B2

Legend has it that Hemi self, wielding a machine rate this timber-pan ered bar during showpiece is a en by Papa ar town. Dress s.com; Hôtel Rit ; ⊘6.30pm-2a

Lonely Planet's Bruges & Brussels

Lonely Planet Pocket Guides are designed to get you straight to the heart of the city.

Inside you'll find all the must-see sights, plus tips to make your visit to each one really memorable. We've split the cities into easy-to-navigate neighbourhoods and provided clear maps so you'll find your way around with ease. Our expert authors have searched out the best of the cities: walks, food, nightlife and shopping, to name a few. Because you want to explore, our 'Local Life' pages will take you to some of the most exciting areas to experience the real Bruges & Brussels.

And of course you'll find all the practical tips you need for a smooth trip: itineraries for short visits, how to get around, and how much to tip the guy who serves you a drink at the end of a long day's exploration.

It's your guarantee of a really great experience.

Our Promise

You can trust our travel information because Lonely Planet authors visit the places we write about, each and every edition. We never accept freebies for positive coverage, so you can rely on us to tell it like it is.

The Best of Bruges & Brussels 123

Bruges & Brussels' Best Walks

Bruges & Brussels' Best ...

Survival Guide 149

QuickStart Guide

Welcome to Bruges & Brussels

Romantic, canal-woven Bruges and buzzing multinational Brussels are both, in their different ways, unmissable. While Brussels dwarfs Bruges in size, both feature boats plying the waterways, serene parks, a web of cycling trails, jumbled market stalls, forward-looking fashions, and museums and galleries packed with home-grown art, from Brueghel masterpieces to Hergé's Tintin. All this plus the finest beer and chocolate in the world.

Canal boat, Bruges
JIM RICHARDSON/NATIONAL GEOGRAPHIC SOCIETY/CORBIS©

Bruges & Brussels
Top Sights

Markt, Bruges (p24)

The beating heart of Bruges, dominated by a high bell tower and artfully lit at night. Climb the tower for a bird's eye view of the city.

Groeningemuseum, Bruges (p46)

A potted history of Belgian art, with an outstanding collection of works by the Flemish Primitives, as well as cityscapes and surrealist pieces.

Burg, Bruges (p26)

Gorgeously gaudy buildings, decorated with shining gilt and clusters of statues. A basilica with a holy relic draws both local worshippers and tourists.

Memlingmuseum, Bruges (p48)

This small collection of devotional paintings, including the gilded Reliquary of St Ursula (above), glows in the dim light of an ancient hospital chapel.

Begijnhof, Bruges (p50)

Take a turn round the tranquil courtyard of the Begijnhof, once a retreat for single and widowed women. Don't miss the absorbing house museum.

Grand Place, Brussels (p68)

Quite simply the most theatrical medieval square in Europe, with a magnificent array of gabled guild houses and a spectacular town hall.

Musées Royaux des Beaux-Arts, Brussels (p88)

Brussels' major gallery covers everything from early Flemish painting to surrealist master Magritte, who has his own dedicated gallery. Don't miss Brueghel's *Fall of Icarus*.

Musée Horta, Brussels (p116)

When Horta designed his own house, he combined technological innovation with high artistry to create a stunning and poetic art nouveau masterpiece.

Parc du Cinquantenaire, Brussels (p104)

The EU district boasts the spacious and leafy Parc du Cinquantenaire, ringed by impressive museums including a military museum and one dedicated solely to cars.

Centre Belge de la Bande Dessinée, Brussels (p70)

A Victor Horta–designed department store hosts this temple to Belgian and international cartoons. Pride of place goes, naturally, to Hergé's beloved Tintin.

Musée des Instruments de Musique, Brussels (p90)

Housed in one of the city's most spectacular art nouveau buildings, this museum takes you on a wonderful audio tour of world music.

Musées Royaux d'Art et d'Histoire, Brussels (p106)

Impressive if a little daunting, this museum has pretty much everything covered, from prehistoric wonders to the swirly splendours of art nouveau.

Bruges & Brussels
Local Life

Insider tips to help you find the real city

Bruges gets a bad rap for being tourist central, but we've located tempting local shops and charming crowd-free back streets, as well as some unexpected windmills. Plus, in Brussels, we'll lead you to hip designer fashion and flea and food markets.

Shopping in Central Bruges (p28)
▶ Obscure beers
▶ Vintage lace

Avid shoppers will find some real gems in Bruges, where you can purchase everything from artisinal cheese to homemade *jenever* to antique crockery. Belgium's famous fashion designers get a look-in too. The stunning Markt is given over to a food market every Wednesday, well worth a look before you head off in search of treasures.

St-Anna Windmills, Bruges (p30)
▶ Windmills
▶ Folk museum

Like Venice, Bruges is a place where it's surprisingly easy to escape the crowds. A gentle wander northeast of the centre reveals some lovely sights: a remarkable church, a folk museum and four very splendid windmills. A couple of old pubs along the way provide suitable beer-based refreshment.

A Sunday Stroll in the Marolles, Brussels (p118)
▶ Markets
▶ Local restaurants

Working-class Brussels lives on in the intriguing Marolles district. The Gare du Midi market is a great place to see how immigration is shaping the city, while at the Jeu-de-Balle flea market you can pick up quirky antiques. It's also a great area for eating and drinking, with some appealing neighbourhood *cafés* and restaurants

Shopping in Ste-Catherine, Brussels (p120)
▶ Cutting-edge fashion
▶ Live jazz

Belgian designers are known worldwide for their bold approach to fashion, and Rue Antoine Dansaert and the surrounding streets make up Brussels' fashion district. Don't be daunted, as shop assistants here are way more laid back than their Milanese counterparts. End a Saturday shop with live jazz at L'Archiduc.

Market stall, Bruges

Window shopping, Brussels

Other great places to experience the city like a local:

Late-Night Eating, Bruges (p37)

Late-Night Tipples, Bruges (p38)

The Belgian Coast, Bruges (p59)

The Vintage, Bruges (p61)

Eating Like a Local, Brussels (p76)

Where to Eat Waffles, Brussels (p78)

Jazz in Brussels (p83)

Recyclart, Brussels (p101)

Maison Antoine, Brussels (p112)

Bruges & Brussels
Day Planner

Day One, Bruges

Stroll past the colonnaded **fish market** (p41) and along the famous canals, or see the city from the water by taking a half-hour **canal cruise** (p53). Get a bird's-eye view of Bruges by climbing to the top of the **Belfort** (p25), then descend to visit the holiest relic in town in the **Heilig-Bloedbasiliek** (p27), before joining the locals lunching at **De Belegde Boterham** (p29).

Admire Belgian art from the Flemish Primitives to the surrealists at the **Groeningemuseum** (p46) and take time out in the courtyard of the serene **Begijnhof** (p50), making sure to visit the little house museum there. Tour the working **De Halve Maan** (p57) brewery where Brugse Zot is created: you'll get to taste a sample en route.

Continue the beer theme with a meal at classy **Den Dijver** (p58), where beer is not only paired with each dish, but is also a key ingredient in the cooking. For yet more Belgian brews, head below ground to tucked-away cellar bar **'t Poatersgat** (p38), or wander the backstreets to find the city's oldest pub, picturesque **Café Vlissinghe** (p38).

Day Two, Bruges

Steer away from the tourist centre and take a morning stroll round the St-Anna district, visiting the **Jeruzalemkerk** (p31), the lace shop, folk museum and the four windmills which enjoy a stately position on a verdant bank. Stop for a pub lunch and a *gueuze* at **De Windmolen** (p31).

Head back to the centre for an artistic highlight of the city: the **Hans Memling paintings** (p48) in the chapel of a medieval hospital; with the same ticket you can see the museum's characterful tiled pharmacy. Escape the crowds again and have a wander in the **Minnewater Park** (p57), before stopping for a drink at local favourite **De Stoepa** (p58).

Have dinner at lively bistro **L'Estaminet** (p29) then catch a classical concert at the modern **Concertgebouw** (p61), or see a movie at arthouse **Cinema Lumière** (p40). Head next door afterwards for a drink at lively **De Republiek** (p38), which is always packed out with young Bruges-dwellers.

Short on time?
We've arranged Bruges and Brussels' must-sees into these day-by-day itineraries to make sure you see the very best of the city in the time you have available.

Day Three, Brussels

The gilded facades encircling Brussels' splendid **Grand Place** (p68) glint in the early morning sun, making it a picturesque spot to kick off a tour of the capital. While here, pop into the city's history museum, **Brussels City Museum** (p69), then stroll through the glass-roofed **Galeries St-Hubert** (p76) to Brussels' **cathedral** (p94) and towards the museums.

Once in the Mont des Arts area, time your trip to the **Musée des Instruments de Musique** (p90) for lunch at its rooftop cafe, housed in a tall and spectacular art nouveau building. If you've got the energy, check out the **Musée BELvue** (p95) for a dose of Brussels history and the **Musées Royaux des Beaux-Arts** (p88) which showcase Belgian art from the Flemish Primitives via Brueghel to Magritte.

Head downhill for dinner and jazz at **Le Cercle des Voyageurs** (p76). Alternatively, take the glass lift outside the colossal **Palais de Justice** (p95) to the Marolles area to dine at one of its renowned restaurants– try **Soul Food** (p96) or **L'Idiot du Village** (p119).

Day Four, Brussels

Browse the Belgian designer boutiques along Rue Antoine Dansaert and the surrounding streets, which showcase big names and hot new talents. Then continue the sartorial theme by heading to the little-known but absorbing costume and lace museum: **Musée du Costume et de la Dentelle** (p74). Have a sandwich lunch at trendy **Le Fonograf** (p80).

Either hop on the tram to Victor Horta's gorgeous art nouveau home-turned-museum, the **Musée Horta** (p116), or instead take the metro east and visit the museums of the EU district, of which the **Musées Royaux d'Art et d'Histoire** (p106) are the standouts, with rich collections of antiquities. Have a stroll round leafy Parc du Cinquantenaire before heading back to town for classic waffles, sprinkled with icing sugar, at **Mokafé** (p78).

Start your evening with a half-and-half at **Le Cirio** (p80) before taking in a traditional puppet show at the quaint **Théâtre Royal de Toone** (p82), or listening to some live music at the **Music Village** (p81). If neither of these options appeals, try a classical concert at Horta-designed **BOZAR** (p100).

Need to Know

For more information, see Survival Guide (p149)

Currency
The euro (€)

Language
French/Dutch

Visas
Not required for US, Canadian, Australian, New Zealand or South African visitors for stays up to six months. European Union nationals can stay indefinitely.

Money
ATMs are widespread. Cash is preferred in small shops; major credit cards in larger ones.

Mobile Phones
European and Australian mobile phones will work. US visitors should check with their service provider. Buy a local SIM card to bring costs down.

Time
Central European Time (GMT/UTC plus one hour)

Plugs & Adaptors
Two-pin plugs; current is 220v. North American visitors require adaptors.

Tipping
Not obligatory, as service charges and VAT are included in hotel and restaurant prices. It's common to round up restaurant bills and taxi fares by a euro or two.

① Before You Go

Your Daily Budget

Budget less than €60
▶ Dorm bed €25–€35
▶ Supermarkets and prix-fixe lunchtime specials
▶ Free national museums, church concerts

Midrange €60–€150
▶ Double room €90
▶ Two-course dinner with glass of wine €30
▶ Jazz concert ticket €15

Top End more than €150
▶ 4-star hotel double room €200
▶ Three-course dinner in top restaurant with wine €60
▶ BOZAR ticket €65

Useful Websites

Lonely Planet (www.lonelyplanet.com) Great for planning

Agenda (www.agenda.be) Nightlife and exhibitions: look out for the trilingual print version too

Visit Brussels (visitbrussels.be) Slick and super-helpful tourist board site

Advance Planning

One month Book accommodation early, particularly for Bruges in high season

Two weeks Book a Brussels Greeter for insider insight (p94)

A few days Buy concert tickets online

② Arriving in Bruges and Brussels

Most travellers to Belgium, whether arriving by air or rail, will generally arrive first in Brussels and then catch onward transport to Bruges.

✈ Arriving by Air

Brussels International Airport (www.brusselsairport.be) is situated 14km northeast of the city. From here, there are regular trains and buses into central Brussels, from where you can catch onward trains to Bruges.

Brussels' second airport, **Brussels South Charleroi Airport** (www.charleroi-airport.com), is 46km southeast of the city and is used mainly by budget airlines including Ryanair. From here, you can catch buses to both Brussels and Bruges.

🚆 Arriving by Train

Most international trains arrive at **Bruxelles-Midi** (South Station), which is the main station for international connections: the Eurostar, TGV and Thalys high-speed trains only stop here. It's too far to walk from Midi to the centre of town - you'll need to take the metro or a taxi.

Most other mainline trains stop in quick succession at **Bruxelles-Midi** (Gare du Midi), **Bruxelles-Central** (Gare Centrale, Central Station) and, except for Amsterdam trains, also at **Bruxelles-Nord** (Gare du Nord, North Station).

Regular trains from Brussels to **Bruges** depart hourly from all three main stations (Bruxelles-Midi, Bruxelles-Central and Bruxelles-Nord).

③ Getting Around

Bruges' train station is 1.5km south of Markt; from here you can catch a taxi or bus into town, or take a scenic 20-minute walk.

Brussels' integrated bus-tram-metro system is operated by STIB/MIVB. Public transport runs from 6am to midnight, after which it's taxi only, except on Friday and Saturday, when 17 Noctis night-bus routes operate twice hourly from midnight to 3am, most starting from Place de Brouckère.

M Tram, Metro and Bus

Brussels metro stations are marked with a white 'M' on a blue background. Lines 1A (northwest–southeast) and 1B (northeast–southwest) share the same central stretch, including useful stops at Bruxelles-Central, Ste-Catherine and Schuman (for the EU Area). Line 2 follows the Petit Ring. Trains run every 10–15 minutes. Underground premetro trams also link Brussels-Nord with Brussels-Midi via the Bourse.

STIB/MIVB tickets are valid across metro, premetro (tram) and bus services. Tickets must be validated before travel, in machines located at the entrance to metro stations, or inside trams and buses.

🚕 Taxi

In Brussels, official taxis (typically black or white) charge €2.40 pick-up plus €1.35 per kilometre. There's a €2 supplement between 10pm and 6am. Waiting costs €25 per hour. Taxes and tips are officially included in the meter price.

🚲 Bicycle

Villo! (🕿 078-051 110; http://en.villo.be; ⏱24hr) is a system of 180 automated stations for short-term bicycle rental in Brussels. You first need to buy a subscription, then charges accumulate and are debited from your credit/bankcard.

Bruges & Brussels
Neighbourhoods

Burg, Markt & the North (p22)
Two stunning interlinked squares are the perfect introduction to the medieval city, and the surrounding lanes are delightful for exploring.

◉ Top Sights

Markt

Burg

Groeningemuseum & the South (p44)
Bruges' major museums are here, including standout collections of the Flemish Primitives, while the Begijnhof is a green retreat.

◉ Top Sights

Groeningemuseum

Memlingmuseum

Begijnhof

Markt
◉ ◉ *Burg*

Groeningemuseum
◉

◉ *Memlingmuseum*

◉ *Begijnhof*

Parc du Cinquantenaire & EU Quarter (p102)

As well as being the gleaming centre of EU power, this district boasts a beautiful park and some fine museums.

⊙ Top Sights

Parc du Cinquantenaire

Musées Royaux d'Art et d'Histoire

Grand Place & Ilôt Sacré (p66)

The geographical heart of Brussels, with dazzling medieval buildings and standout restaurants, theatres and music venues.

⊙ Top Sights

Grand Place

Centre Belge de la Bande Dessinée

Royal Quarter Museums (p86)

This stately district has a compelling cluster of museums, some lovely green spaces, and the city's best chocolatiers.

⊙ Top Sights

Musées Royaux des Beaux-Arts

Musée des Instruments de Musique

Centre Belge de la Bande Dessinée

Grand Place

Musée des Instruments de Musique

Parc du Cinquantenaire

Musées Royaux des Beaux-Arts

Musées Royaux d'Art et d'Histoire

Explore
Bruges

Rooftops in Bruges
BRUCE ESBIN/GETTY IMAGES©

Explore

Burg, Markt & the North

If you set out to design a fairy-tale medieval town it would be hard to improve on central Bruges. Picturesque cobbled lanes and dreamy canals link photogenic market squares lined with soaring towers and historic churches. The only downside is the crush of tourists, especially in summer. Wander to the north and east of the centre though, and you'll discover a different, more enigmatic Bruges.

The Sights in a Day

☀ Start your day with a coffee on the **Markt** (p24), then climb the **Belfort** (p25) to get your bearings on the city and beyond. Head to the **Burg** (p26), exploring the Renaissancezaal (Renaissance Hall) within the **Brugse Vrije** (p27), and deciphering the colourful murals of the **Gotische Zaal** (Gothic Hall) in the **Stadhuis** (p27). Then go and see the city's most sacred relic, housed in the **Heilig-Bloedbasiliek** (p27). For lunch, sample the wares of one of the two *frites* sellers on the Markt.

☀ The **Jan Van Eyckplein** is one of the city's most gracious squares, adorned with a statue of the artist, abutted by a canal and ringed by cafes. Look out for the ornate **Tolhuis** (toll house) building, as well as the handsome townhouses to either side of the water. Nearby, the grandiose **Koninklijke Stadsschouwburg** (p40) is a handsome 19th-century theatre.

☽ For more immersion in old Bruges, have a hearty supper and a beer at **Café Vlissinghe** (p38), a fixture here since 1515. Further quintessential Bruges beer experiences can be had at cellar bar **'t Poatersgat** (p38). Before heading back to your accommodation, return to the Markt to see the square in all its floodlit glory.

For a local's day in Bruges, see p28.

◉ **Top Sights**

Markt (p24)

Burg (p26)

◯ **Local Life**

Shopping in Central Bruges (p28)

St-Anna Windmills (p30)

♥ **Best of Bruges**

Drinking Beer
De Garre (p39)

't Poatersgat (p38)

Café Vlissinghe (p38)

Cambrinus (p39)

Markets
Markt (p24)

Vismarkt (p41)

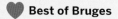

Getting There

🚌 From the **train** station it takes around 20 minutes to walk to the centre of Bruges.

🚌 Any **bus** marked 'Centrum' runs to the Markt.

Top Sights
Markt

Flanked by medieval-style step-gabled buildings, this wonderfully dramatic open market square is Bruges' nerve centre. Horse-drawn carriages clatter between open-air restaurants and camera-clicking tourists, watched over by a statue of Pieter De Coninck and Jan Breydel, the leaders of the Bruges Matins. It's undeniably one of the most touristy parts of town, but visually it's still stunning and shouldn't be missed; there's more of a local feel on Wednesday when a food market takes centre stage.

Map p32, B7

Markt

Don't Miss

The Belfort

The symbol of Bruges is its Unesco-listed 13th-century **Belfort** (Belfry; adult/concession/child €8/6/5; ⊙9.30am-5pm, last tickets 4.15pm), rising a lofty 83m above the Markt. The 366 steps bring you past the treasury, a triumphal bell and a 47-bell manually-operated carillon which still chimes across the city. Once at the top, look out across the red-tiled rooftops towards the wind turbines and giant cranes of Zeebrugge. Visitor numbers are limited to 70 at once, which can cause queues at peak times.

Historium

Still under wraps at the time of writing, the **Historium** (☎050 27 03 11; www.historium.be) occupies a neo-Gothic building on the northern side of the square. Taking visitors back to 1435, it is an immersive multimedia experience, claiming to be more medieval movie than museum. A love story gives narrative structure, and you can nose around Van Eyck's studio, amongst other historic experiences.

The market

Appropriately enough, this historic market square is still the location for a major food market held on Wednesday mornings. Locals and tourists mix to purchase cheeses, sausages, spit-roasted meat, fruit, veg and plants. Authentic waffles are sold from a van, and the Belfort looms picturesquely over proceedings.

The Eiermarkt

Immediately to the north and adjoining the Markt, this little square can be identified by a stone column surmounted by lions. It's ringed by *cafés* and bars, and is a marginally cheaper and less frenetic place for a coffee or a drink than the Markt itself.

☑ **Top Tips**

▸ If you're visiting lots of sights, consider buying a Bruges City Card (p35).

▸ Be sure to visit the square at night, when it's quieter and beautifully floodlit.

▸ Carriage tours (€39 for up to five people) depart from the Markt and take 30 minutes, including a pit stop at the Begijnhof (p50).

▸ In summer, aim to make a carriage trip between 6pm and 7pm when most day-trippers have left town and Bruges' buildings glow golden in the sun's late rays.

✖ **Take a Break**

There are numerous tourist-orientated *cafés* to choose from on the square, or go for takeaway *frites* (from €2.25) and hot dogs (from €3) sold from two green vans on the Markt.

Top Sights
Burg

One short block east of the Markt, the less theatrical but still enchanting Burg has been Bruges' administrative hub for centuries. It also hosted the St-Donatian Cathedral till 1799, when it was torn down by antireligious zealots. A modern addition is the mildly baffling Toyo Ito pavilion, a geometric contemporary artwork at the square's tree-filled centre. With your back to it you can admire the southern flank of the Burg, incorporating three superb interlinked facades which glow with gilded detail.

Map p32, C7

Burg

Don't Miss

Brugse Vrije

This eye-catching building, with early baroque gabling and golden statuettes, was once the palace of the 'Liberty of Bruges', the territory that was ruled from Bruges from 1121 to 1794. The building still houses city offices, but you can visit the **Renaissancezaal** (Renaissance Hall; Burg 11a; ⏱9.30am-noon & 1.30-4.30) to admire its remarkable 1531 carved chimney piece. An incredibly detailed oak carving depicts Emperor Charles V, flanked by his grandfathers, Ferdinand of Aragon and Maximilian of Austria, both of whom sport flattering codpieces.

Stadhuis

The beautiful 1420 **Stadhuis** (City Hall; Burg 12) has a fanciful facade covered with replica statues of the counts and countesses of Flanders (the originals were torn down in 1792). Inside, an audioguide leads you upstairs to the astonishing **Gotische Zaal** (Gothic Hall; adult/concession €4/3; ⏱9.30am-5pm). Few rooms anywhere achieve such a jaw-dropping first impression as this dazzling hall with its polychrome ceiling, hanging vaults and romantic historical murals.

Heilig-Bloedbasiliek

The Stadhuis' western end morphs into the **Heilig-Bloedbasiliek** (Basilica of the Holy Blood; Burg 5; ⏱9.30-11.50am & 2-5.50pm Apr-Sep, 10-11.50am & 2-3.50pm Thu-Tue, 10-11.50am Wed Oct-Mar), which takes its name from a phial supposedly containing a few drops of Christ's blood that was brought here after the Crusades. Upstairs is a colourful chapel, where the relic is hidden behind a flamboyant silver tabernacle. Also upstairs is the basilica's treasury, where you'll see the jewel-studded reliquary in which the phial is mounted on Ascension Day for the Heilig-Bloedprocessie. Downstairs is the basilica's 12th-century Romanesque chapel, a meditative place almost devoid of decoration.

☑ Top Tips

▶ Do take the (free) audio guide for the Gotische Zaal – it explains the narrative behind the murals and sheds light on the city's history.

▶ The Holy Blood relic in the basilica is brought out for veneration at 2pm daily – respectful and quiet visitors are welcome.

▶ Like the Markt, the Burg is at its most tranquil and beautiful in the early evening and at night.

▶ Just south of the Burg and across the bridge, don't miss the lovely colonnaded 1821 Vismarkt (fish market; p41), which still accommodates fish stalls most mornings, along with trinket sellers later in the day.

✗ Take a Break

Try tiny De Garre (p39), a beer lovers' favourite, tucked away on an alley between the Markt and the Burg.

Local Life
Shopping in Central Bruges

There are times when central Bruges can feel like a melée of waffle stands and *frites* stalls. It's worth remembering, though, that this is indeed a real place, where discerning locals do their shopping, eating and drinking. Beyond the touristy facade, there are some real finds if you're looking for interesting beers, cheeses and charcuterie, as well as fashion, lace and bric-a-brac.

❶ Market shop on the Markt
The Markt is, generally speaking, tourist central, crammed with horse-driven carriages and tour groups. But on Wednesday mornings it's a genuinely local experience, when an excellent food market takes centre stage. It's ideal if you're planning a picnic, or simply want some fresh fruit to counter the heavy Belgian grub. Speciality cheeses and sausages are amongst the offerings.

2 Pick up fine food at the Diksmuids Boterhuis

This gorgeously traditional **grocery** (Geldmuntstraat 23; ⏲10am-12.30pm & 2-6.30pm) is now surrounded with mainstream boutiques, but it has been here since 1933. Decked out with red and white gingham flounces and featuring a ceiling hung with sausages, it purveys cheeses, honey, cold meat and mustard.

3 Women's fashion at L'Heroine

The cool concrete exterior of **L'Heroine** (Noordzandstraat 32; ⏲10.30-6pm Mon-Sat) stands out amongst the chains. Here you'll find established Belgian designers Dries Van Noten and Ann Demeulemeester as well as young talents like Christian Wijnants. They stock beautiful silk print dresses, asymmetrical tailoring and sumptuous scarves and drapes – staff can help you combine pieces for a strong, idiosyncratic look. It's less daunting than it looks, and you're welcome to browse.

4 Lunch at De Belegde Boterham

Duck the tourist crowds at this popular **lunch spot** (☎050 34 91 31; Kleine St Amandsstraat 5; ⏲noon-4pm, closed Sun) for well-heeled locals. The monochrome boutique styling is a bit formal, but it's a friendly place and the food – soups, sandwiches and large salads – is excellent, with fresh ingredients and tasty dressings. Good coffee too.

5 Best beers at Bacchus Cornelius

When locals buy run-of-the-mill beer, they do so at supermarkets. But if they want a special tipple, they come to **Bacchus Cornelius** (☎050 34 53 38; Academiestraat 17; ⏲1pm-6.30pm). There's a cornucopia of 450 beers and rare *gueuzes*, as well as *jenevers* and liqueurs flavoured with elderflower, cranberries and cherries. Ask the shop owner if you can try her homebrewed silky smooth *jenever*, made with real chocolate. The two pianos are there for shoppers to play, and an open fire in winter adds to the cosy vibe.

6 Madam Mim for bric-a-brac

A must for lovers of vintage, adorable **Madam Mim** (Hoogstraat 29; ⏲11am-6pm Wed-Mon) sells quirky clothes handmade from vintage fabrics by shopowner Mim herself, as well as '60s crockery, cut glass, glorious hats and '70s kids' clothes. You can also pick up antique lace for a fraction of the cost it goes for elsewhere.

7 Dinner at L'Estaminet

With its dark timber beams, low lighting and convivial clatter, **L'Estaminet** (☎050 33 09 16; Park 5; snacks/pasta from €6/8; ⏲11.30am-11pm Tue-Sun, 4pm-11pm Thu) scarcely seems to have changed since it opened in 1900. It's primarily a drinking spot, but also serves time-honoured dishes such as spaghetti bolognaise with a baked cheese crust. Summer sees its loyal local following flow out onto the front terrace.

Local Life
St-Anna Windmills

The district of St-Anna provides a delightful breather away from central Bruges, as well as an insight into the industrious past of the district. The handmade lace industry is still just about alive – you can see lace being made at the Kantcentrum, while the folk museum explores the working lives of past residents. Four handsome windmills frame a spectacular vista over the town.

❶ **Visit the Museum voor Volkskunde**

The appealing **Museum voor Volkskunde** (Museum of Folklore; Balstraat 43; adult/concession €2/1; ⊙9.30am-5pm Tue-Sun, De Zwarte Kat closed 11.45am-2pm) presents visitors with 18 themed tableaux illustrating Flemish life in times gone by (a 1930s sweetshop, a hatter's workshop, a traditional kitchen etc). It's a static

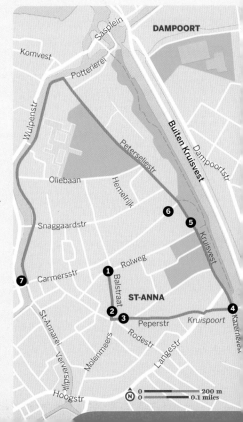

affair, but the setting is an attractive *godshuis* and the time-warp museum *café*, **De Zwarte Kat**, charges just €1.25 for a beer. Temporary exhibits upstairs are often worth a look.

❷ Shop for lace at 't Apostelientje

Once you locate the scenic backstreets of Bruges you'll find there's scarcely a soul in sight. Take a wander up Balstraat to this quaint little **shop** (📞050 33 78 60; Balstraat 11; ⏰9.30am-12.15pm & 1.15-5pm Wed-Sat, 1pm-5pm Tue, 10am-1pm Sun). The delicate garments and gifts on sale are made from beautiful and authentic lace, handmade by two sisters and their mother; the husband of one of the sisters makes the wooden bobbins. An unusual opportunity to buy the real Bruges deal lace-wise.

❸ See lace created at the Kantcentrum

Past the dramatic **Jeruzalemkerk** (Map p32, D5; Peperstraat 1), the **Kantcentrum** (Lace Centre; www.kantcentrum. com; Peperstraat 3a; adult/child €2.50/1.50; ⏰10am-noon & 2-6pm Mon-Fri, to 5pm Sat) displays a collection of lace in a row of interlinked old cottages. The centre's main attraction is that (afternoons only) you can watch bobbin lace being made by informal gatherings of experienced lace-makers and their students who gather to chat and work here. Once you've seen how mind-bendingly fiddly the process is, you'll swiftly understand why handmade lace is so very expensive.

❹ View the Medieval Walls

The fortified gate-tower **Kruispoort** (on Langestraat) is an impressive isolated remnant of the former city wall.

❺ Visit the Windmills

From the 13th century through to the 19th century, Bruges' ramparts were graced with *molens* (windmills); ambling along the canal bounding the eastern side of the city takes you through pretty parkland past Bruges' four remaining examples. You can visit two of the four, which still grind cereals into flour today, and which each house a little museum: the 18th-century **St Janshuismolen** (Kruisvest; adult/concession €2/1.50; ⏰9.30am-12.30pm & 1.30-5pm Tue-Sun May-Sep), and the **Koeleweimolen** (Kruisvest; adult/concession €2/1.50; ⏰9.30am-12.30pm & 1.30-5pm Tue-Sun Jul & Aug).

❻ Break for a drink at De Windmolen

Take a break at this quaint corner **café** (📞050-339 739; Carmersstraat 135; beer/snacks/pasta from €1.80/4.50/8.50; ⏰10am-late Mon-Thu, to 3am Fri & Sun) with a sunny terrace overlooking one of the St-Anna windmills. It's mainly patronised by locals, and offers a good low-key location to sample the local brews.

❼ Follow canalside Potterierei

Wind your way back to the centre along scenic Potterierei, where statues of the Madonna adorn every corner. Look out for the small lever bridge that's reminiscent of Amsterdam.

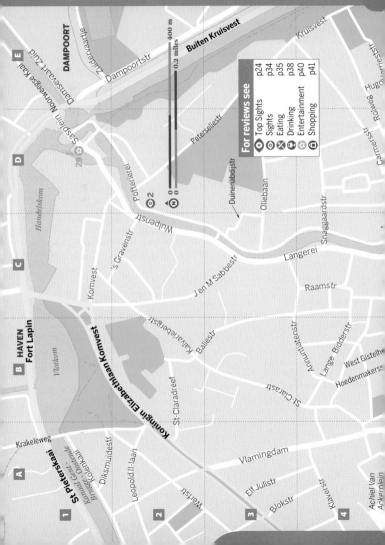

DAMPOORT

Buiten Kruisvest

400 m

0.2 miles

For reviews see

Top Sights	p24
Sights	p34
Eating	p35
Drinking	p38
Entertainment	p40
Shopping	p41

HAVEN
Fort Lapin

St Pieterskaai

Sights

Jeruzalemkerk
CHURCH

1 ⦿ Map p32, D5

This extraordinary 15th-century structure is supposedly based upon Jerusalem's Church of the Holy Sepulchre. It's a macabre monument with a gruesome altarpiece covered in skull motifs and an effigy of Christ's corpse tucked away in the rear chapel. The black-marble tomb of Anselm Adornes contains only his heart; he was murdered in Scotland in 1483. To see inside you'll need to purchase a ticket to the attached Kantcentrum (p31). (Peperstraat 1)

Jeruzalemkerk

OLV-ter-Potterie
MUSEUM

2 ⦿ Map p32, D2

Entry to this small historical church-hospital complex is free with a St-Janshospitaal museum ticket. Ring the bell to gain entry and you'll find yet more fine 15th- to 16th-century art. The lushly baroque church section houses the reliquary of St-Idesbaldus and a polychrome wooden relief of Mary breastfeeding baby Jesus. In more prudish later centuries the virgin's nipple received a lacy camouflage, rendering the scene bizarrely impractical. (Potterierei 79; adult/concession €2/1; ☉ 9.30am-12.30pm & 1.30-5pm)

Crowne Plaza Hotel
EXCAVATIONS

3 ⦿ Map p32, C6

In the 1990s, when excavating the foundations of the Crowne Plaza Hotel, workers literally hit a wall. It belonged to 10th-century St-Donaas church, which later became a cathedral. Construction was allowed to proceed, provided that the remains were accessible to the public at no cost. It's occasionally closed for hotel conferences, but otherwise you're free to descend at any time to see old maps, paintings and tombs. (Burg 10)

Choco-Story
MUSEUM

4 ⦿ Map p32, C6

A highly absorbing chocolate museum tracing the cocoa bean back to its role as an Aztec currency. Learn about choco-history, watch a video on cocoa production and sample a praline that's made as you watch (last demonstration 4.45pm). (www.choco-story.be; Wijnzakstraat 2 (St-Jansplein); adult/child €7/4; ⏱10am-5pm)

Frietmuseum

MUSEUM

5 Map p32, B6

This museum follows the history of the potato from ancient Inca gravesites to the Belgian fryer, though the result is somewhat less than gripping. The entry fee includes a discount-token for the basement *frituur* that immodestly claims to fry the world's ultimate potato chips. (☎050 34 01 50; www.frietmuseum.be; Vlamingstraat 33; adult/concession/child €6/5/4, frituur fries €2; ⏱10am-5pm, frituur 11am-3pm, both closed Christmas–mid-Jan)

 Top Tip

Bargain Bruges

If you're visiting more than a couple of sights, invest in a **Bruges City Card** (www.bruggecitycard.be; 48h/72h €35/€40), which gives entry to all the main city museums, plus various attractions including private ventures such as Choco-Story and De Halve Maan brewery. You'll also score a canal boat ride (which shouldn't be missed, however cheesy it may seem), as well as discounts on bicycle rental, concerts, films and theatre.

Eating

De Stove

GASTRONOMY $$

6 ✗ Map p32, B7

Just 20 seats keep this gem intimate. Fish caught daily is the house speciality, but the monthly changing menu also includes the likes of wild boar fillet on oyster mushrooms. Everything, from the bread to the ice cream, is homemade. Despite perennially rave reviews, this calm, one-room family restaurant remains friendly, reliable and inventive, without a hint of tourist-tweeness. (☎050 33 78 35; www.restaurantdestove.be; Kleine St-Amandsstraat 4; mains €19-33, menu €42, with wine €58; ⏱noon-1.30pm Sat & Sun & 7pm-9pm Fri-Tue)

Den Gouden Karpel

SEAFOOD $

7 ✗ Map p32, C7

Takeaway or eat in, this sleek little cafe/bar is a great location for a jumpingly fresh seafood lunch, right by the fish market. Crab sandwiches for €3.50, smoked salmon salad for €13, shrimp croquettes for €10.50 and oysters €9.50. (☎050 33 33 89; www.dengoudenkarpel.be; Vismarkt 9-11; ⏱11am-6pm Tue-Sat)

De Bottelier

MEDITERRANEAN $$

8 ✗ Map p32, A6

Decorated with hats and old clocks, this adorable little restaurant sits above a wine shop overlooking a delightful slice of canal-side garden. Diners are predominantly local; reservations are wise. (☏050 33 18 60; www.debottelier.com; St-Jakobsstraat 63; pasta/veg dishes from €8.80/13.50, other mains from €16; ☺lunch & dinner Tue-Fri, dinner only Sat)

De Karmeliet   RESTAURANT $$$

9 ✖ Map p32, D6

Chef Geert Van Hecke's intricate combinations, such as stuffed courgette with poached quail eggs, caviar, king crab and mousseline champagne, have earned him a trio of Michelin stars. The setting is slightly austere, but gourmands will be too busy swooning to notice. Lunch menus are a good deal. Book well ahead, especially for weekends. (☏050 33 82 59; www.dekarmeliet.be; Langestraat 19; mains €55-95, menus €80-170; ☺lunch & dinner)

Chagall   BELGIAN $$

10 ✖ Map p32, A7

Checked olive banquettes, candles, shelves cluttered with knick-knacks and an upright piano make you feel like you're dining in a family home. Seafood, including several variations on eel and the usual *moules* (mussels), is Chagall's specialty, but it also does daily specials such as wild boar stew, and good deals on two- and three-course menus. (☏050 33 61 12; St-Amandsstraat 40; 2/3 courses €18/26; ☺closed Wed)

Interior of the Bauhaus (p40)

Gran Kaffee De Passage   BISTRO $

11 ✖ Map p32, A8

A mix of regulars and travellers from the adjoining hostel give this candle-lit, art deco–style bistro one of the best atmospheres in town. Its hearty traditional dishes, such as *stoverij* (local meat in beer sauce), are basic but filling – and a bargain. (☏050 34 02 32; www.passagebruges.com; Dweersstraat 26-28; mains €5-10; ☺6-11pm)

Merveilleux Tearoom   CAFE $

12 ✖ Map p32, A7

Elegant marble-floored tearoom on a cobbled passage near the Markt. Coffee comes with a dainty homemade biscuit and sometimes a little glass of strawberry ice cream or chocolate mousse. Pretty cakes and tea are on offer too. (☎050 61 02 09; www.merveilleux.eu; Muntpoort 8; high tea €10, mains €15-22; ☺10am-6pm)

Da Vinci ICE CREAM $

13 ❌ Map p32, A7

Not being able to choose between the 40 luscious flavours of freshly made ice cream at this *gelateria* is a good thing, as it means you'll be offered small spoonfuls of free samples to help you decide (of course, that might just make the decision harder). In high summer it stays open until 11pm. (☎050 33 36 50; Geldmuntstraat 34; scoops €1.30; ☺closed mid-Nov–Feb)

Tous Paris SELF-CATERING $

14 ❌ Map p32, A8

If you and your arteries need a break from waffles and fries, this gourmet grocer offers a welcome alternative by way of fresh salads, quiches and made-to-order sandwiches on white or wholegrain baguettes. (☎050 33 79 02; Zuidzandstraat 31; snacks €3-8; ☺closed Wed & Thu)

In 't Nieuwe Museum BELGIAN $$

15 ❌ Map p32, E7

So called because of the museumlike collection of brewery plaques, money boxes and other mementos of *café* life

adorning the walls, this family-owned local favourite serves five kinds of *dagschotel* (dish of the day) for lunch (€7 to €12.50), and succulent meat cooked on a 17th-century open fire in the evenings. Specials include veggie burgers, eel dishes, ribs, steaks and creamy *vispannetje* (fish casserole). (☎050 33 12 22; Hooistraat 42; mains €10-25; ☺noon-2pm & 6-10pm Thu-Tue, closed Sat lunch)

◯ Local Life
Late-Night & Early-Morning Eating

If your stomach demands more than just chips or kebabs after 11pm, try the effortlessly elegant, open-kitchened restaurant **Christophe** (p60), which serves until 1am. Or, before 3am, you could tuck into typical Flemish fare at the cosily historic **'t Gulden Vlies** (Map p32, C6; ☎050 33 47 09; www.tguldenvlies.be; Mallebergplaats 17; mains €14-22, 2-/3-course menu €16/27; ☺7pm-3am Wed-Sun). Most restaurants lining the Markt offer breakfasts with a view from €7, but check carefully what's included before sitting down. If you just want coffee and a croissant, the cheapest deal is at bakery **Panos** (Map p52, A2; Zuidzandstraat 29; coffee/croissant €1.80/1.10; ☺7am-6.30pm Mon-Sat, 11am-6.30pm Sun).

Est Wijnbar
TAPAS $

16 Map p32, C7

This attractive little wine bar – the building dates back to 1637 – is an especially lively spot on Sunday nights, when you can catch live jazz, blues and occasionally other musical styles from 8.30pm. It's also a pleasantly informal supper spot, with raclette, pasta, snacks and salads on the menu, and tasty desserts. (050 33 38 39; www.wijnbarest.be; Braambergstraat 7; mains €9.50-12.50, tapas €3.50-9.50; 4pm-midnight Wed-Sun;)

't Ganzespel
BELGIAN $

17 Map p32, E6

Providing a truly intimate eating experience in a lovely old gabled building, the owner serves classic Belgian dishes such as meatballs and *kalfsblanket* (veal in a creamy sauce) as well as pasta dishes. (050 33 12 33; www.ganzespel.be; Ganzenstraat 37; main, salad & soup €9.50; 6pm-10pm Fri-Sun)

Drinking

't Poatersgat
PUB

18 Map p32, B5

Look carefully for the concealed hole in the wall and follow the staircase down into this cross-vaulted cellar glowing with ethereal white lights and flickering candles. 't Poatersgat (which means 'the Monk's Hole' in the local dialect) has 120 Belgian beers

on the menu, including a smashing selection of Trappists. (Vlaamingstraat 82; 5pm-late)

Café Vlissinghe
PUB

19 Map p32, D5

Luminaries have frequented Bruges' oldest pub since it first opened its doors in 1515. The interior is gorgeously preserved with wood panelling and a wood-burning stove, but in summer the best seats are in the shady garden where you can play *boules* in between sips. Nice snacks such as croques, and cheese and meat platters. (050 34 37 37; Blekersstraat 2; 11am-midnight Wed-Sat, 11am-7pm Sun)

De Republiek
PUB

20 Map p32, A6

Set around a courtyard comprising characterful brick buildings, this big,

---

Local Life
Late-Night Tipples

If you're still going strong after midnight, head to **Vino Vino** (Map p32, B6; 050 34 51 15; Grauwwerkersstraat 15; 6pm-late Tue-Sat). This candle-lit bar with beamed ceilings plays blues music and serves inexpensive tapas and snacks. For other late-night options, head round the corner onto Kuiperstraat; a good place to start is **'t Zwart Huis** (Map p32, B6; the Black House; Kuipersstraat 23), which featured in the movie *In Bruges*.

Café Vlissinghe

buzzing space is super-popular with Bruggelingen (Bruges locals). DJs hit the decks on Friday and Saturday nights and there's a range of well-priced meals, including vegetarian options, available until midnight, plus a long cocktail list. (www.derepubliek.be; St-Jakobsstraat 36; ⏱11am-late)

De Garre   PUB

21 🍺 Map p32, B7

Nowhere else on the planet serves the fabulous 11% Garre draught beer, which comes with a thick floral head in a glass that's almost a brandy balloon. This hidden two-floor *estaminet* (tavern) also stocks dozens of other fine Belgian brews including the remarkable Struise Pannepot (€3.50).

A good mix of locals and visitors prop up the bar. (📞050 34 10 29; Garre 1; ⏱noon-midnight)

Cambrinus   BEER PUB

22 🍺 Map p32, C6

Traditional Belgian and Italian-inspired snacks, as well as good-value lunch and dinner menus, help soak up the hundreds of varieties of beer available at this 17th-century brasserie/pub. It's very much on the tourist trail, so you may struggle to find a seat on weekend evenings, but don't be put off: the atmosphere is lively and welcoming. (📞050 33 23 28; www.cambrinus.eu; Philipstockstraat 19; ⏱11am-11pm Sun-Thu, 11am-late Fri & Sat)

Opus Latino

CAFÉ

23 🔴 Map p32, C7

A modernist *café* with weather-worn terrace tables right on the waterfront, where a canal dead-ends beside a Buddha-head fountain. Access is via the easily missed shopping passage that links Wollestraat to Burg, emerging near the Basilica of the Holy Blood. (☎050 33 97 46; beer/snacks/tapas from €2.20/8.50/6; ⏱11am-11pm Thu-Tue)

Bauhaus

BAR

24 🔴 Map p32, E5

One of Belgium's most popular hangouts for young travellers, this virtual backpacker 'village' incorporates a bustling hostel, apartments, a nightclub, internet cafe and a little chill-out room that's well hidden behind the reception and laundrette section at Langestraat 145. The bar-restaurant (**Sacré Coeur**) is excellent except when you're trying to sleep above it. Take bus 6 or 16 from the train station. (☎050 34 10 93; www.bauhaus.be; Langestraat 145; 🛜)

Charlie Rockets

PUB

25 🔴 Map p32, C6

A lively bar in vaguely Hard Rock Café style, featuring a big cinema projector, table football and a pool table. Music (live on winter Fridays) plays till late, reverberating through the sturdy dormitories upstairs. (☎050 33 06 60; www.charlierockets.com; Hoogstraat 19; ⏱8am-4am)

Entertainment

Cinema Lumière

CINEMA

26 ⭐ Map p32, A6

Just a couple of blocks back from the Markt, this slightly scruffy but very appealing art-house cinema screens a well-chosen program of foreign films in their original languages. It's also the home of the Cinema Novo Film Festival, an indie event held each March which showcases Asian, African and Latin American films. You can eat and drink next door at **De Republiek**. (☎050 34 34 65; www.lumiere. be; St-Jakobsstraat 36)

Retsin's Lucifernum

CLUB

27 ⭐ Map p32, C6

This former Masonic lodge is draped in flags, scaffolding and body parts. Ring the bell on a Sunday night and hope you're invited inside, where an otherworldly candle-lit bar may be serving potent rum cocktails and you'll be serenaded with live Latin music. Or maybe not. It's always a surprise. (☎0476 35 06 51; www.lucifernum. com; Twijnstraat 6-8; admission incl drink €6; ⏱6-10pm Sun only)

Koninklijke Stadsschouwburg

THEATRE

28 ⭐ Map p32, B6

Cultuurcentrum Brugge coordinates theatrical and concert events at several venues, including this majestic 1869 theatre. Opera, classical concerts,

> ### Understand
> ### *In Bruges*
> -
> The city hit the big screen when the 2008 Sundance Film Festival premiered the action-comedy, *In Bruges*. Written and directed by Irish playwright Martin McDonagh, it stars Colin Farrell and Brendan Gleeson, who play hit men ordered by their boss (Ralph Fiennes) to hide out in Bruges during the pre-Christmas frenzy. The tagline 'shoot first, sightsee later' gives you an idea of the plot – made more bizarre by encounters with a string of surreal Felliniesque characters. It's peppered with hilariously obscene and un-PC invective about the quaintly pretty city which, to their credit, the people of Bruges seem to find as funny as everyone else.

theatre and dance are on offer; out the front is a statue of Papageno, from Mozart's *The Magic Flute*. (📞050 44 30 60; Vlamingstraat 29)

Du Phare
LIVE MUSIC

29 ⭐ Map p32, D1

Tucked into the remains of one of Bruges' original town gates, this off-the-beaten-track tavern is best known for its live blues/jazz sessions – check the website for dates. It also serves up huge portions of couscous (and offers free bread, a rarity in Belgium). Bus 4 stops out the front. (📞050 34 35 90; www.duphare.be; Sasplein 2; ⏱kitchen 11.30am-3pm & 6pm-midnight, bar 11.30am-late, closed Tue)

Entrenous
CLUB

30 ⭐ Map p32, E5

This has been a long time coming for the youth of Bruges: a real nightclub in the centre of the city. A very youthful crowd packs out their DJ nights,

gigs and after-parties. (📞050 34 10 93; www.bauhauszaal.be; Langestraat 145; ⏱10pm-late Fri &/or Sat)

Joey's Café
LIVE MUSIC

31 ⭐ Map p32, A8

These days Joey's is run by Stevie, who performs with local band Cajun Moon; consequently, this dark, intimate bar is a gathering spot for Bruges' musos. There's a live music festival in August, or you can chill out with a creamy Stevie cocktail any time. (📞050 34 12 64; Zuidzandstraat 16A; ⏱11.30am-late Mon-Sat)

Shopping

Vismarkt
MARKET

32 🔒 Map p32, C7

At the colonnaded Vismarkt (fish market), fishmongers have been selling their North Sea produce for centuries. These days only a few vendors set up on the cold stone slabs, but it's still worth a gander. Join locals buying snacks such as *maatjes* (herring fillets). On weekends, the Vismarkt and nearby Dijver are taken over by antique and bric-a-brac stalls. (Steenhouwersdijk; ⏱8am-1pm Tue-Sat)

De Reyghere Reisboekhandel

BOOKS

33 🛍 Map p32, B7

Poring over the huge range of travel guides in English, Dutch and French at this specialised travel bookshop is guaranteed to give you itchy feet. Its adjoining sister store has general nonfiction, novels and English newspapers. (☎050 33 34 03; Markt 12; ⏱9.30am-noon Tue-Sat & 2pm-6pm Mon-Sat)

De Biertempel

BEER

34 🛍 Map p32, B6

Specialist beer shop, where you can even pick up a well-priced bottle of Westvleteren. (☎050 34 37 30; Philipstockstraat 7; ⏱10am-6pm)

Rombaux

MUSIC

35 🛍 Map p32, C6

Here since 1920, this large and extremely classy family-run music shop specialises in classical music, jazz, world music, folk and Flemish music, and is the kind of place where you can browse for hours. Expert staff

The art of lace-making

Understand
Laced up

There are two main ways of making lace (*kant*/*dentelle* in Dutch/French). **Needlepoint lace** (*naaldkant*) uses a single thread to embroider a pattern on a piece of cloth or paper that will eventually be discarded. Originally Italian, the technique was perfected in Brussels, and the classic needlepoint stitch is still known as 'corded Brussels'. In contrast, **bobbin lace** (*kloskant*) creates a web of interlinked threads using multiple threaded-bobbins meticulously twisted using a maze of hand-placed pins. It's an astonishingly fiddly process, believed to have originated in 14th-century Bruges. Some of the finest known handmade samples, made using hundreds of bobbins, originated in Binche, while **Chantilly**, an originally French sub-form using black cotton, was for years a noted speciality craft of Geraardsbergen. To save time and avoid errors, 19th-century Brussels manufacturers came up with **cut-thread lace** in which a series of smaller bobbin-lace details are sewn together to create larger pieces. The most typical styles were **Rosaline**, where little rose details were often pearl-embroidered, and **Duchesse**, with flower-and-leaf motifs. These days much lace-making is mechanised, but the handmade craft can still be seen at Bruges' Kantcentrum (p31); for where to buy lace see p30.

are on hand to help. (☎050 33 25 75; Mallebergplaats 13; ☺2-6.30pm Mon, 10am-12.30pm & 2-6.30pm Tue-Fri, 10am-6pm Sat)

Olivier Strelli
FASHION

36 🔒 Map p32, B6

Prominent corner boutique given over to Belgium's best-known fashionista. Born in the Congo to Italian and Greek Jewish parents, Strelli trained as a textile designer before becoming a designer of sophisticated but funky ready-to-wear fashion for men and women. Colours tend to the bold side: lemon yellow, pistachio, purple and coral. (☎050 34 38 37; Eiermarkt 3; ☺10am-6:30pm Mon-Sat)

2-Be
FOOD, DRINK

37 🔒 Map p32, C7

Occupying a 15th-century Gothic mansion, this commercial emporium stocks a tantalising array of artisan chocolates, wines, *jenevers*, conserves, sweets, biscuits and other Belgian goodies including a vast selection of beers, such as local Brugse Zot, which you can try at their canalside *café*. Ask staff to fill you in on resident ghost Perez de Malvenda, the former Spanish mayor whose house this once was. (☎050 61 12 22; www.2-be.biz; Wollestraat 53; ☺10am-7pm)

Explore

Groeningemuseum & the South

To locals' bemusement, at least some of Bruges' 3.2 million annual visitors mistake the city for an open-air museum, particularly in this area where historic buildings, galleries and churches are densely clustered. True, Bruges' Gothic architecture, willow-lined waterways and market squares are almost impossibly quaint. But beyond the souvenir shops you'll find cosy backstreet bars, young artisans and a palpable sense of history.

The Sights in a Day

☼ Start your day by immersing yourself in art, first at the **Groeningemuseum** (p46) for an overview of Belgian art history, then at the **Memlingmuseum** (p48), a wonderful and historic showcase for six masterworks by Hans Memling. Your museum ticket also allows you to see the ancient hospital building, in addition to a 17th-century **pharmacy** (p49); well worth a look.

☼ Break for lunch at **Den Dijver** (p58), where food is cooked in the country's finest beer. Here you're well placed to make a post-prandial and leisurely **boat cruise** (p53): seeing the city from a canal is an essential Bruges experience. Wander down to the **begijnhof** (p50), whose courtyard is an oasis of calm, and be sure to visit the austerely beautiful **house museum** (p51) there. In good weather have a stroll to the **Minnewater Park** (p57) and relax amongst the flowerbeds.

☾ For a pleasant and laidback supper on a quiet backstreet try **De Stoepa** (p58), where decent bistro food is served. After dinner, take a stroll around this residential area for a taste of 'real' Bruges. Finish with a classical concert at the **Concertgebouw** (p61), Bruges' concession to modernity.

👁 **Top Sights**

Groeningemuseum (p46)

Memlingmuseum (p48)

Begijnhof (p50)

💗 **Best of Bruges**

Best for the Flemish Primitives
Groeningemuseum (p46)

Memlingmuseum (p48)

Best Museums
't Begijnhuisje (p51)

Diamantmuseum (p54)

Best Green Spaces
Minnewater (p57)

Begijnhof (p50)

Getting There

🚶 From the train station it takes around 20 minutes to **walk** to the centre of Bruges.

🚌 Any **bus** marked 'Centrum' runs to the Markt, from where it's a short stroll south to the Groeningemuseum.

Top Sights
Groeningemuseum

A candidate for Bruges' most celebrated art gallery which, while not enormous, packs in an astonishingly rich collection of Flemish Primitive and Renaissance works. There are some intriguing early images of the city of Bruges itself, as well as an eye-popping Hieronymous Bosch. More meditative works include Jan Van Eyck's radiant *Madonna with Canon George Van der Paele* (1436) and Hans Memling's *Moreel Triptych* (1484). Later artists also get a look in, including superstar symbolist Fernand Khnopff; plus there's a canvas each from Magritte and Delvaux.

Map p52, D2

www.brugge.be

Dijver 12

adult/concession €8/6

🕑9.30am-5pm Tue-Sun

Madonna with Canon George Van der Paele (1436) by Jan Van Eyck

Don't Miss

City as Patron

The gallery gets under way with absorbing images of the city commissioned by its merchant patrons. A map – more like an aerial view – shows 15th-century Bruges in every detail, from spinning windmills to tall ships in the harbour. Gerard David's grisly *Judgement of Cambyses* (1498) also features the cityscape.

Flemish Primitives

Things take off artistically in the Flemish Primitives room, crammed with works by Jan van Eyck, Roger van der Weyden, Hans Memling and Gerard David. These pieces depict the conspicuous wealth of the city with glitteringly realistic artistry. Typical is the Madonna by the Master of the Embroidered Foliage, where the rich fabric of the Madonna's robe meets the 'real' foliage at her feet with exquisite detail. Jan van Eyck's wonderful portraits also reflect these traits, as well as adding a dimension of psychological realism.

Townscapes and Landscapes

Visions of the city surface again in this room, with picturesque scenes by Jan Anton Garemijn, as well as Auguste van de Steene's austere view of the market square.

Flemish Expressionism

These works from the 1920s show the influence of cubism and German expressionism on Flemish artists – most striking are Constant Permeke's earth-coloured depictions of peasant life in *Pap Eaters* and *The Angelus*. Two further rooms also cover the modern period, ending with works from the '60s and '70s which show the influence of arch-surrealist Magritte.

☑ Top Tips

▶ As with most Belgian attractions, the museum is closed on Monday.

▶ You can visit for free with the Bruges Card (p35).

▶ The museum is justifiably popular, so arrive as early as possible at busy times of year.

▶ If you're short on time, focus on works by the Flemish Primitives, which are the high point of the museum.

▶ Dazzle other gallery-goers with your knowledge: you'll notice the work of the 'Primitives' is pretty sophisticated – the name derives from the Latin *primus* (first) as the artists were the first to adopt new painting techniques.

✗ Take a Break

A short walk along the canal from the museum brings you to stylish Den Dijver (p58), serving top-quality Belgian cuisine.

Top Sights
Memlingmuseum

In the restored chapel of a 12th-century hospital building with superb timber beamwork, the St-Janshospitaal shows various historical medical implements and medically themed paintings, but is best known for the Memlingmuseum which exhibits six glowing masterpieces by 15th-century artist Hans Memling, including the enchanting *Reliquary of St Ursula*. Memling was born in Frankfurt, but spent most of his painting career in Bruges. Your ticket also covers a visit to the hospital's restored 17th-century *apotheek* (pharmacy), located in the same complex of buildings.

Map p52, C2

☏ 050 44 87 43

Mariastraat 38, south of the Markt

€8/€6

🕙 9.30am-5pm Tue-Sun

The St-Janshospitaal, home of the Memlingmuseum

Don't Miss

The Memling paintings

The old hospital chapel is dedicated to a small but priceless collection of works by Hans Memling, which glow in the dim light. Largest is the triptych of St John the Baptist and St John the Evangelist, commissioned by the hospital church as its altarpiece. Look out for St Catherine (with spinning wheel) and St Barbara, both seated at the feet of the Virgin. Memling's secular portrayals are just as engrossing, such as the delicate *Portrait of a Young Woman* (1480), in which the subject's hands rest on the painted frame of her portrait.

The Reliquary of St Ursula

This gilded oak reliquary looks like a mini Gothic cathedral, painted by Memling with scenes from the life of St Ursula, including highly realistic Cologne cityscapes. The devout Ursula was a Breton princess betrothed to a pagan prince. She agreed to marry him on the condition she could make a pilgrimage to Rome (via Cologne) with 11,000 virgins. All were murdered on the return journey by the king of the Huns, along with Ursula and her betrothed.

St-Janshospitaal artefacts

Lofty St-Janshospitaal has been elegantly restored to show off both the exposed beams of the 12th-century building and an array of artefacts relating to the museum. The latter include tortuous-looking medical implements, hospital sedan chairs and a gruesome 1679 painting of an anatomy class.

☑ Top Tips

▶ Buy a Bruges City Card (p35) if you're seeing a number of museums in the city – it also offers discounts on travel, tickets and some restaurants.

▶ The museum shop has an excellent in-depth guide to the exhibits and paintings (€12.50).

▶ Though it's not the main event, the 17th-century *apotheek* is worth a look. The glazed cloisters of the building you walk through to enter it are very attractive, and the pharmacy itself is a beautiful tiled space with rows of jars and a pendulum clock.

▶ Take a peek into the Trustees Room, adjoining the pharmacy, which is lined with portraits of bewigged and beruffed trustees.

✕ Take a Break

Head down Mariastraat till it turns into Katelijnestraat, to enjoy the veggie offerings of De Bron (p59).

Top Sights
Begijnhof

Bruges' delightful *begijnhof* dates from the 13th century. Although the last *begijn* has long since passed away (see p56), today residents of the pretty, whitewashed garden complex include a convent of Benedictine nuns. Despite the hordes of summer tourists, the *begijnhof* remains a remarkably tranquil haven, and in spring a carpet of daffodils adds to the quaintness of the scene. Just inside the main entrance, 't Begijnhuisje is a typical *begijnhof* house now converted into an endearing four-room museum.

Map p52, B4

admission free

⊘ 6.30am-6.30pm

Begijnhof

Don't Miss

't Begijnhuisje

This charming 17th-century house is now a domestic **museum** (Begijnhof, Wijngaardstraat; adult/child/senior €2/€1/€1.50; ☺10am-5pm Mon-Sat, 2.30pm-5pm Sun). In the rustic kitchen with its blue and white Delft tiles you'll see a Louvain stove which extends into the room from the hearth so that people can sit round it. The sitting room displays black Chantilly lace (see p43), while the austere bedroom has a portrait showing a traditional *begijn* costume. The dining room features a simple wooden cupboard which served as a pantry, china store and pull-out dining table; beyond the house is a simple stone cloister with a well.

Church of the Beguinage

The baroque church features a flamboyant high altar, 17th-century choir stalls, and chubby putti adorning the choir screen. Outside, tall elm trees frame the view of the whitewashed houses, and despite the occasional crowds there's still a secluded, villagelike air to the place.

The Minnewater

Known in English as the 'Lake of Love', the charming nearby park around the Minnewater really does give this area a romantic quality, and there are plenty of sheltered paths and benches to retreat to on a sunny day. In Bruges' medieval heyday, this is where ships from far and wide would unload their cargoes of wool, wine, spices and silks.

☑ Top Tips

▶ Outside the *begijnhof*'s 1776 gateway bridge lies a tempting array of terraced restaurants and waffle peddlers: handy if you want a snack nearby, though prices are on the high side.

▶ Look out for the horse fountain over the bridge – the sculpted horses' heads spurt water, allowing carriage-drivers to fill buckets and give their horses a drink.

▶ The Minnewater is a good location for a picnic, so you might want to bring food with you.

▶ Photograph the *begijnhof* at dawn or dusk for maximum tranquility and good light.

▶ For more information on Bruges' *begijn* see p56.

✗ Take a Break

Stroll down a tranquil backstreet to delightful De Stoepa (p58), for bistro food and a pleasant hippie vibe.

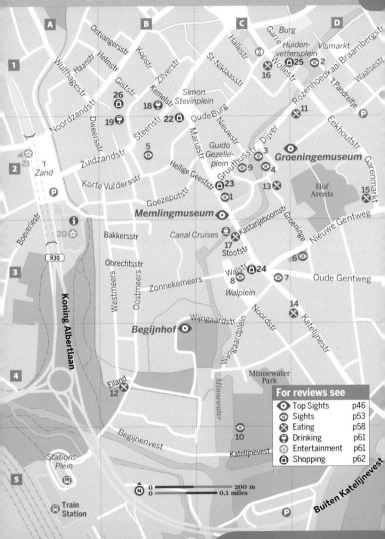

For reviews see

◉	Top Sights	p46
◉	Sights	p53
✖	Eating	p58
🍷	Drinking	p61
★	Entertainment	p61
🔒	Shopping	p62

0 — 200 m
0 — 0.1 miles

Sights

Onze-Lieve-Vrouwekerk CHURCH

1 ⊙ Map p52, C2

This large, somewhat sober 13th-century church sports an enormous tower. The church is best known as the location of Michelangelo's serenely contemplative *Madonna and Child* statue (1504); there's also the *Adoration of the Shepherds* by Pieter Pourbus. In the church's apse, the **treasury section** displays some splendid 15th- and 16th-century artworks, plus the fine stone-and-bronze tombs of Charles the Bold and his daughter, Mary of Burgundy. (Church of Our Lady; Mariastraat; treasury section adult/concession €2.50/2; ⏱9.30am-4.50pm Mon-Sat, 1.30-4.50pm Sun)

Canal Tour BOAT TOUR

2 ⊙ Map p52, D1

Taking a canal tour is a must. Yep, it's touristy, but what isn't in Bruges? Viewing the city from the water gives it a totally different feel than by foot. Cruise down Spiegelrei towards Jan Van Eyckplein and it's possible to imagine Venetian merchants entering the city centuries ago and meeting under the slender turret of the Poortersloge building up ahead. Boats depart roughly every 20 minutes from jetties south of the Burg, including Rozenhoedkaai and Dijver, and tours last 30 minutes. Expect queues in summer. (adult/child €7.60/3.40; ⏱10am-6pm Mar–mid-Nov)

Arentshuis MUSEUM

3 ⊙ Map p52, C2

With your Groeningemuseum ticket, admission is free to this stately 18th-century patrician house displaying the powerful paintings and dark-hued etchings of Frank Brangwyn (1867–1956), a Bruges-born artist of Welsh parentage. His images of World War I – he was an official war artist – are particularly powerful. (Dijver 16; adult/concession/child €2/1/free; ⏱9.30am-5pm Tue-Sun)

Hof Arents PARK

4 ⊙ Map p52, C2

Behind the Arentshuis, Hof Arents is a charming little park where a hump-backed pedestrian bridge, **St-Bonifaciusbrug**, crosses the canal for idyllic views. Generally nicknamed Lovers' Bridge, it's where many Bruges citizens steal their first kiss. Privileged guests staying at the guesthouse **Nuit Blanche** get the romantic moonlit scene all to themselves once the park has closed. (admission free; ⏱7am-10pm Apr-Sep, till 9pm Oct-Mar)

St-Salvatorskathedraal CHURCH

5 ⊙ Map p52, B2

Stacked sub-towers top the massive central tower of 13th-century St-Saviour's Cathedral. In daylight the construction looks somewhat dour, but once floodlit at night it takes on a mesmerising Escheresque fascination. The cathedral's interior is vast but feels oddly plain despite a selection of antique tapestries. Beneath the tower, a glass floor reveals some painted graves, and there's a passingly interesting **treasury** displaying 15th-century brasses and a 1559 triptych by Dirk Bouts. (Steenstraat; treasury adult/concession €2/1; ⊘2-5.45pm Mon, 9am-noon & 2-5.45pm Tue-Fri, 9am-noon & 2-3.30pm Sat & Sun, treasury 2-5pm Sun-Fri)

Godshuis St-Jozef & De Meulenaere
BUILDING

6 ◉ Map p52, D3

One of the delights of wandering around Bruges is the chance of coming across a complex of *godshuizen* (almshouses). One of the town's most charming and central *godshuizen* is Godshuis St-Jozef & De Meulenaere. Enter through the large black doors. (Nieuwe Gentweg 24)

Diamantmuseum
MUSEUM

7 ◉ Map p52, C3

While Antwerp is now the centre of the diamond industry, the idea of polishing the stones with diamond 'dust' was originally pioneered in Bruges. This is the theme developed by this slick museum which also displays a lumpy, greenish 252-carat raw diamond and explains how the catchphrase 'diamonds are forever'

JONATHAN SMITH/GETTY IMAGES©

Canal boats

Understand
Flemish Primitives

Belgium's celebrated art heritage blossomed in 15th-century Bruges with painters now known collectively as the **Flemish Primitives**. It may seem an odd choice of term given that not all were Flemish and their work was anything but primitive – the term actually derives from the Latin *primus*, meaning first, an indication of their innovative and experimental approach. They pioneered a technique of painting in oil on oak boards, adding thin layers of paint to produce jewel-bright colours and exquisite detail.

Their radiant use of colour and intricately detailed depictions of secular subjects greatly influenced the course of European art. Especially notable was **Jan Van Eyck** (c 1390–1441), who became remarkably wealthy combining painting with a lucrative sinecure as royal valet to the powerful Dukes of Burgundy. Van Eyck lived in Bruges; the Groeningemuseum (p46) has some particularly superb canvases by him, including an intimate portrait of his wife. Other major names include **Rogier Van der Weyden** (c 1400–94) and Dutchman **Gerard David** (c 1460–1523), both predominantly Bruges-based.

Another star of the period was **Hans Memling** (c 1440–94). It's thought that he came to Bruges from Cologne aged around 25; already a fully trained artist, he may have trained for a period in Brussels under Rogier van der Weyden. Memling swiftly became a favourite amongst the city's merchant patrons, and also began an association with St John's Hospital which resulted in the commissioning of the glowing religious works now displayed in the Memlingmuseum (p48). Here you can also see his St Ursula reliquary, one of the city's most important treasures.

The Primitives' contemporary **Hieronymous Bosch** (c 1450–1516) worked mainly in the Netherlands, though the distinction between Dutch and Flemish painting is somewhat artificial, since before the late 16th century Belgium and the Netherlands were simply known as the Low Countries and artists frequently moved from one royal court or town to another. Bosch's most fascinating paintings are nightmarish visual parables filled with gruesome beasts and devilish creatures often devouring or torturing agonised humans. Bosch's work had obvious influences on the great 16th-century Flemish painter **Pieter Brueghel the Elder**. Works by both Bosch and Brueghel can be seen in the Groeningemuseum (p46).

Understand
Begijnhoven & Godshuizen

In the 12th century, large numbers of men from the Low Countries embarked on Crusades to the Holy Land and never returned. Their now unchaperoned women-folk often felt obliged to seek security by joining a religious order. However, joining a convent required giving up one's worldly possessions and even one's name. A middle way, especially appealing to relatively wealthy widows, was to become a *begijn* (*béguine* in French). These lay sisters made Catholic vows including obedience and chastity, but could maintain their private wealth. They lived in a self-contained **begijnhof** (*béguinage* in French): a cluster of houses built around a central garden and church, surrounded by a protective wall. Land (normally at the outskirts of town) was typically granted by a pious feudal lord, but once established these all-female communities were self-sufficient. Most had a farm and vegetable garden and made supplementary income from lace-making and from benefactors who would pay the *begijnen* to pray for them.

In the 16th century, Holland's growing Protestantism meant that most Dutch *begijnhoven* were swept away. In contrast, Spanish-ruled Flanders was gripped by a fervently Catholic counter-reformation that reshaped the *begijn* movement. Rebuilt *begijnhoven* became more hospice-style institutions with vastly improved funding. From 1583 the Archbishop of Mechelen decreed a standardised rulebook and a nunlike 'uniform' for *begijnen,* who at one point comprised almost 5% of Flanders' female population.

A century ago some 1500 *begijnen* remained in Belgium, but now only one remains, Marcella Pattyn in Kortrijk. Kortrijk's is one of 14 Flanders *begijnhoven* on the Unesco World Heritage List. Each is beautifully preserved albeit these days lived in by ordinary townsfolk, with Bruges' being one of the most idyllic.

Looking somewhat similar to *begijnhoven* but usually on a smaller scale are **godshuizen** (almshouses), typically featuring red-brick or whitewashed shuttered cottages set around a tiny enclosed garden. Originally built by merchant guilds for their members or by rich sponsors to provide shelter for the poor (and to save the sponsors' souls), these days they're great places to peacefully unwind if you dare to push open their usually closed doors. Bruges has a remarkable 46 *godshuizen*.

started as a De Beers marketing campaign. **Diamond-polishing demonstrations** cost €3 extra. (Diamond Museum; ☏ 050 34 20 56; www.diamondmuseum.be; Katelijnestraat 43; adult/senior/student €7/6/5; ⏲ 10.30am-5.30pm, demonstrations 12.15pm & 3.15pm)

Brouwerij De Halve Maan

BREWERY

8 ◉ Map p52, C3

Founded in 1856, this is the last family *brouwerij* (brewery) in central Bruges. Multilingual **guided visits**, lasting 45 minutes, depart on each hour. They include a tasting, and can sometimes be rather crowded. Alternatively you can simply sip one of their excellent *Brugse Zot* (Bruges Fool, 7%) or *Straffe Hendrik* (Strong Henry, 9%) beers in the appealing brewery *café*. (☏ 050 33 26 97; www.halvemaan.be; Walplein 26; tours €6.50; ⏲ 45-min tours hourly 11am-4pm Apr-Sep, 11am & 3pm Oct-Mar; brasserie 10.30am-6pm, closed 2 weeks mid-Jan)

Gruuthuse

MUSEUM

9 ◉ Map p52, C2

Takes its name from the flower and herb mixture (*gruut*) that was used to flavour beer before the cultivation of hops. The romantic heraldic entrance in a courtyard of ivy-covered walls and dreaming spires is arguably more interesting than the rambling, somewhat unsatisfying decorative-arts exhibits within. The unusual view from the upstairs oratory window into the treasury-apse of the Onze-Lievevrouwekerk is worth a look. (Dijver 17; adult/concession €6/5; ⏲ 9.30am-5pm Tue-Sun)

Minnewater

CANAL

10 ◉ Map p52, C5

Known in English as the Lake of Love, the Minnewater harks back to Bruges' medieval heyday. This waterway was a dock where ships from as far afield as Russia came laden with cargoes of wool, wine, spices and silks and left loaded with Flemish cloth.

CHRIS PANCEWICZ/ALAMY ©

De Halve Maan Brewery

Eating

Den Dijver

BELGIAN **$$**

11  Map p52, D1

Not only are the seasonal dishes at this elegant restaurant individually paired with beers, they're also cooked in Belgium's favourite nectar. One delicious example is the hare, turnip and cranberry ravioli cooked in Oude Gueuze, which is served with a Petrus Winterbier. Three-, four- and five-course menus can be ordered, with a beer accompanying each course. There's also the option of pairing with wines, but that would be missing the point. (☑050 33 60 69; www.dijver.be; mains €19-26, 3-/4-/5-course menu €46/56/73, incl beers €56/68/89; ⊙noon-2pm & 6.30-9.30pm Fri-Mon)

De Stoepa

BISTRO **$$**

12  Map p52, B4

A gem of a place in a peaceful residential setting with a slightly hippy/Buddhist feel. Oriental statues, terracotta-coloured walls, a metal stove and wooden floors and furniture give a homey but stylish feel. Best of all, though, is the leafy terrace garden. Tuck into the upmarket bistro-style food. (☑050 33 04 54; www.stoepa.be; Oostmeers 124; ⊙noon-2pm & 6pm-midnight Tue-Sat, noon-3pm & 6pm-11pm Sun)

Minnewater Park (p57)

Den Gouden Harynck

EUROPEAN $$$

13 🍴 Map p52, C2

Behind an ivy-clad facade, this uncluttered Michelin-starred restaurant garners consistent praise and won't hurt the purse quite as severely as certain better-known competitors. A lovely location: both central and secluded. (📞050 33 76 37; www.dengoudenharynck.be; Groeninge 25; mains €38-45, set lunch menu €35, 3-/4-course menus €74/89; ⏱lunch & dinner Tue-Sat)

Christophe

BELGIAN $$

15 🍴 Map p52, D2

A cool late-night bistro with marble table-tops and a decent range of Flemish staples including fresh Zeebrugge shrimps. An excellent late-nighter. (📞050 34 48 92; www.christophe-brugge.be; Garenmarkt 34; mains €17-30; ⏱6pm-1am Thu-Mon)

De Bron

VEGETARIAN $

14 🍴 Map p52, D3

By the time this glass-roofed restaurant's doors open, a queue has usually formed outside, full of diners keen to get vegetarian fare direct from *de bron* (the source). Dishes are available in small, medium and large, and there are some delicious soups, such as pumpkin. Vegans are catered for on request. (📞050 33 45 26; Katelijnestraat 82; ⏱lunch Mon-Fri; 🍴)

Bye Bye Bruges – the Belgian Coast

If the crowds of Bruges prove a little too much, make like a local and take a quick trip to the coast. A rapid train trip (or 50-minute bike ride) brings you to Belgium's 65km of coastline.

Highlights along the coast include the seafront promenade at the former glamour resort, now busy fishing port, **Ostend** (www. inenuitoostende.be); Belgium's most captivating beach resort at **Belle Époque De Haan** (www. dehaan.be); high-rise-dominated **Knokke** (www.knokke-heist.be); the superb **Paul Delvaux Museum** (📞058 52 12 29; www.delvauxmuseum. com; Delvauxlaan 42; admission €8; ⏱10.30am-5.30pm Tue-Sun Apr-Sep, Thu-Sun Oct-Dec, closed Jan-Mar) in **St Idesbald**; and a cute theme park in De Panne, **Plopsaland** (📞058 42 02 02; www.plopsaland.be; De Pannelaan 68; admission incl rides €32; ⏱10am-5.30pm Apr-Jun, 10am-7pm Jul & Aug, 10am-5.30pm Wed, Sat & Sun Sep & Oct).

Coastal trams (De Kusttram; 📞070 22 02 20; www.dekusttram.be; 1/3 day ticket €5/10; ⏱departing every 15min, 5:30am-11pm; 2hrs) trundle almost the entire coast, stopping at 70 seaside towns and villages between Knokke in the northeast and De Panne in the southwest. Hourly **trains** connect Bruges with Knokke (€3, 15 minutes), Ostend (€3.30, 15 minutes), Zeebrugge (€2.40, 10 minutes) and De Panne (€7.40, one hour; change at Lichtervelde).

Understand
Belgian Brews

Belgian beer is much more than a recipe for a good night out. Beer is to Belgium what wine is to neighbouring France – something to be savoured slowly, appreciating each brew's individual characteristics and flavours. Appreciating them all could take a while: it's estimated that up to 1000 different beers are brewed nationwide. Each beer has its own unique glass embossed with the beer's logo (marking the level where the head starts) and is specially shaped to enhance the taste and aromas, meaning pouring techniques vary.

While monks in France are renowned for winemaking, in Belgium they're devoted to beer. Smooth gold- and dark-coloured Trappist beers – packing a 6% to 12% alcohol content – have been made for centuries by Trappist (Cistercian) monks. These days, the monks' average age is 70, and there are few new recruits, prompting fears for the beers' future. For now, three abbeys still brew in Flanders.

And, in the same way that France has champagne, Belgium has its traditional vintage, the lambic (*lambiek* in Dutch). Like champagne, these sparkling beers take up to three years to make. The secret is wild microorganisms that inhabit the cold air around the beer, causing spontaneous fermentation. The most popular lambic is the cider-style *gueuze* (pronounced 'gerze'). They're an acquired taste, but beginners can try fruit lambics that are sweetened with more palatable cherry or raspberry.

Easier to wash down are pale, cloudy white beers (*witbier* in Dutch, *bière blanche* in French), such as Bruges' Brugs Tarwebier. These are great iced with lemon in warm weather, unlike many of the country's beers, which are actually best drunk at room temperature.

Belgium also boasts golden ales, abbey beers (strong, full-flavoured ales, like Leffe, using original abbey recipes), Vlaams Rood ('Flemish Red' beers, aged in wooden barrels), and sour-tasting Oud Bruin ('Old Brown' beers that blend young and old brews, with a secondary fermentation in the bottle).

Bistro Arthies

BISTRO $$

16 Map p52, C1

This bistro is managed by Arthies, an interior designer who looks like a dashing Gothic Billy Connolly. He uses a projected clock, giant black flower bowls and stylishly whacky lamps to create an ambience that's eccentric yet fashion conscious. There's an all-day €18 menu. (☏050 33 43 13; www.arthies. com; Wollestraat 10; mains/mussels from €19/21; ⏰11.30am-10pm Wed-Mon)

De Proeverie TEAROOM $

17 ✖ Map p52, C3

A chintzy but appealing tearoom serving a variety of teas, gloopy hot chocolate, milkshakes and indulgent homemade sweets including crème brûlée, chocolate mousse and *merveilleux*. (📞050 33 08 87; www.deproeverie.be; Katelijnstraat 5-6; ⏰9.30am-6pm)

Drinking

't Brugs Beertje PUB

18 🍺 Map p52, B1

Legendary throughout Bruges, Belgium and beyond for its hundreds of Belgian brews, this cosy brown *café* is filled with old advertising posters and locals who are part of the furniture. It's one of those perfect beer-bars with smoke-yellowed walls, enamel signs,

---

Q Local Life

The Vintage

For something a bit different, have a drink at **The Vintage** (Map p52, B2; 📞050 34 30 63; www.thevintage.be; Westmeers 13; 11am-1am Mon, Tue & Thu, till 2am Fri & Sat, noon-1am Sun). Unusually hip for Bruges, it has a chilled out '60s/'70s vibe, and a vintage Vespa hanging from the roof. The sunny terrace is a nice spot for a Jupiler. Be warned: the theme parties can be quite raucous.

---

hop-sprig ceilings and knowledgeable staff to help you choose from a book full of brews. (Kemelstraat 5; ⏰4pm-1am Thu-Tue)

Cafédraal BAR

19 🍺 Map p52, B2

Attached to an upmarket seafood restaurant this remarkable aperitif/cocktail bar has an enclosed tree-shaded garden and displays bottles in gilt 'holy' niches. Despite being illuminated by luminous fish and hanging 'hams', it somehow manages to feel suavely classy rather than ridiculous. (📞050 34 08 45; www.cafedraal.be; Zilverstraat 38; beer/wine/cocktails from €2.80/5/10; ⏰6pm-1am Tue-Thu, to 3am Fri & Sat)

Entertainment

Concertgebouw CONCERT HALL

20 ⭐ Map p52, A3

Bruges' stunning 21st-century concert hall is the work of architects Paul Robbrecht and Hilde Daem and takes its design cues from the city's three famous towers and red bricks. Theatre, classical music and dance are regularly staged. Tickets can be purchased from the tourist office, which is situated at street level. (📞050 47 69 99; www.concertgebouw.be; 't Zand 34; tickets from €10)

Cactus Muziekcentrum

LIVE MUSIC

21 ⭐ Map p52, A2

Though small, this is the city's top venue for contemporary and world music, regularly featuring live bands and international DJs. It also organises festivals, including July's **Cactus Music Festival** (www.cactus festival.be), held in the Minnewater park at the southern edge of the old city. (📞 050 33 20 14; www.cactusmusic.be; Magdalenastraat 27)

Shopping

Chocolate Line

CHOCOLATE

22 🔒 Map p52, B2

Bruges has 50 chocolate shops, but just five where chocolates are hand-made on the premises. Of these, the Chocolate Line is the brightest and best. Wildly experimental flavours by 'shock-o-latier' Dominique Persoone include bitter Coca-Cola, as well as black olive, tomato and basil; they also sell pots of chocolate body paint (complete with brush). (📞 050 34 10 90; www.thechocolateline.be; Simon Stevinplein 19; per kg €50; 🕙10am-6pm)

JUNKO CHIBA/GETTY IMAGES©

Chocolates

Zucchero

SWEETS

23 Map p52, C2

A fabulous sweet shop with eye-popping fuschia decor. It sells umpteen varieties of fudge and candies, plus ice cream to go. Check out the candy sticks being hand-chopped by the young owners. (☎050 33 39 62; www.confiserie-zucchero.be; Mariastraat 18; ⏱10am-6pm Tue-Sat, 11am-6pm Sun)

De Striep

COMICS

24 Map p52, C3

Look for Thibaut Vandorselaer's wonderful illustrated guides at this colourful comic shop. There's a comprehensive collection in Dutch, French and English. (☎050 33 71 12; Katelijnestraat 42; ⏱10am-12.30pm & 1.30-7pm Tue-Sat, 2-6pm Sun)

Mille-Fleurs

HOMEWARES

25 Map p52, C1

A cornucopia of Flemish tapestries machine-made near Wetteren. Worth a browse if you want to take a piece of Belgium home with you. They also sell throws, tapestry cushions, runners, doilies, bags and purses. (☎050 34 54 54; www.millefleurstapestries.com; Wollestraat 33)

Zilverpand

SHOPPING CENTRE

26 Map p52, B1

Shopping gallery located between Steenstraat and Noordzandstraat, mostly comprising mid-range fashion boutiques.

Explore
Brussels

Worth a Trip

Grand Place
JONATHAN SMITH/GETTY IMAGES©

Explore

Grand Place & Ilôt Sacré

Brussels' heart beats in the Grand Place, which is ringed by gold-trimmed, gabled houses and flanked by the 15th-century Gothic town hall. The cobblestones were laid in the 12th century, when it was used as a market-place; the names of the surrounding lanes still evoke herbs, cheese and poultry. In the 1960s these lanes were threatened with demolition, prompting proprietors to establish the 'free commune' of Ilôt Sacré.

The Sights in a Day

Where else to start your day but the **Grand Place** (p68), identifying the splendid guild houses and visiting the **Brussels City Museum** (p69). Next, head to the **Musée du Costume et de la Dentelle** (p74) to see handmade Brussels lace bedecking lovely historic gowns and shawls. Break for lunch at funky **Le Fonograf** (p80) or, if you're feeling flush, at **La Maison du Cygne** (p79).

Take a turn around the glorious **Galeries St-Hubert** (p76) in the footsteps of Victor Hugo. Cartoon fans will love the **Centre Belge de la Bande Dessinée** (p70), while architecture buffs can marvel at the Horta-designed department store in which it is housed. Have a pre-dinner beer at the irresistible **Théâtre Royal de Toone** (p82).

Enjoy a leisurely supper and listen to some live piano at **Le Cercle des Voyageurs** (p76) – while you're here, take a short detour to see the small but still unmistakable **Manneken Pis** (p74). Head to the **Music Village** (p81) for more live jazz, or order a half-and-half at **Le Cirio** (p80). Return to the Grand Place at night, to see it in floodlit glory.

👁 Top Sights

Grand Place (p68)

Centre Belge de la Bande Dessinée (p70)

💜 Best of Brussels

Best for Haute Cuisine
Café-Restaurant de l'Ogenblik (p76)

La Maison du Cygne (p79)

Sea Grill (p79)

Best Live Music Bars
Le Cercle des Voyageurs (p76)

Le Fonograf (p80)

Music Village (p81)

Art Base (p82)

Best Cinemas
Actor's Studio (p82)

Cinéma Galeries (p82)

Getting There

M This central area is easily accessed via **metro** stations De Brouckère, Gare Centrale and Rogier, and **premetro** station Bourse.

Top Sights
Grand Place

The magnificent Grand Place is one of the world's most unforgettable urban ensembles. Oddly hidden, the enclosed cobblestone square is only revealed as you enter on foot from one of six narrow side alleys: Rue des Harengs is the best first approach. The focal point is the magnificently spired 15th-century city hall, but each of the fabulous antique guildhalls (mostly 1697–1705) has a charm of its own. Most are unashamed exhibitionists adorned with fine baroque gables, gilded statues and elaborate guild symbols.

Map p72, C6

M Gare Centrale or
🚊 Bourse

Guildhalls on the Grand Place

Don't Miss

Hôtel de Ville
Built between 1444 and 1480, the splendid **Hôtel de Ville** was almost the only building on the Grand Place to escape bombardment by the French in 1695. The creamy stone facade is covered with Gothic gargoyles, while the intricate tower soars 96m, topped by a gilded statue of St-Michel, Brussels' patron saint.

Maison du Roi
This fanciful feast of neo-Gothic arches, verdigris statues and mini-spires is bigger, darker and nearly 200 years younger than the surrounding guild-houses. Once a medieval bread-market, nowadays it houses the **Brussels City Museum** (☏02-279 43 50; www.brucity.be; adult/concession €3/2.50; ⏱10am-5pm Tue-Sun; Ⓜ Gare Centrale or 🚋 Bourse), featuring old maps, architectural relics and paintings. Don't miss Pieter Brueghel the Elder's 1567 *Cortège de Noces* (Wedding Procession), and the 760-odd costumes – including an Elvis suit – belonging to Manneken Pis (p74).

Houses & Guildhalls
Highlights amongst the Grand Place's guildhous-es, listed by street number and guild, include: **La Louve** (5; Archers) – the golden phoenix signifies the rebirth of the Grand Place after the bombard-ment; **Le Cornet** (6; Boatmen) has a stern-shaped gable; **Le Cygne** (9; Butchers) hosted Karl Marx in 1847; **L'Arbre d'Or** (10; Brewers) features climbing hop plants – the basement houses a small Brewery Museum (p75).

Dukes' of Brabant Mansion
The mansion consists of six 1698 houses behind a single palatial facade reworked in 1882. Had the imperial governor had his way after 1695, the whole square would have looked rather like this.

☑ **Top Tips**

▶ Tours depart from the tourist office daily: 10am for a bike tour (p148) or 3pm for a city walking tour with the same company.

▶ There are 45-minute guided **tours** (Hôtel de Ville; €25; ⏱3pm Wed year-round, 10am & 2pm Sun Apr-Sep) of the Hôtel de Ville in English.

▶ Alive with classic *cafés*, the square takes on different auras at different times. Try to visit more than once and don't miss a look at night when the scene is magically (and taste-fully) illuminated.

▶ There's a flower market on Monday, Wednesday and Friday mornings.

▶ The Grand Place also hosts everything from Christmas fairs to rock concerts to the extraor-dinary biennial 'flower carpet' (August).

✖ **Take a Break**

Take time out for biscuits, tea and ice cream at historic Dandoy (p78), just off the Grand Place.

Top Sights
Centre Belge de la Bande Dessinée

Belgium's national Comic Strip Centre is a studious look at the evolution of comics: how they're made, seminal artists and their creations, and contemporary comic-strip artists. Even if you're not excited by the 'ninth art', do peep inside Victor Horta's 1906 light-filled glass-and-steel textile warehouse in which the museum is housed. Few interpretive signs are in English; ask at the ticket desk to borrow an English-language booklet. There is also a comprehensive shop selling comics, and a pleasant cafe.

Map p72, E3

☏ 02-219 19 80

www.comicscenter.net

Rue des Sables 20

adult/concession €8/6

🕙 10am-6pm Tue-Sun

Ⓜ Rogier

Centre Belge de la Bande Dessinée

Don't Miss

The Invention of the Comic Strip

This exploration of the history of the ninth art goes right back to mosaics, and makes a compelling case that the manuscripts of medieval monks – with their divided story strips and speech bubbles – were the first cartoons. The evolution continues via Hokusai's vivid sketches of wrestlers through to the picture stories of 19th-century New York newspapers.

The Museum of the Imagination

This gallery focuses on Belgium's favourite cartoon character: Tintin, created by the great Hergé. It posits Tintin as a visually blank 'everyman' who can transform himself into a granny, a turbaned Indian or a white-bearded sage. Volatile Captain Haddock is by contrast a volcano of uncontrolled emotion, while the narrative is often sparked by the misunderstandings and bizarre actions of Professor Calculus. Amongst other Belgian artists explored in less depth, you may want to pause over the little blue creatures created by Peyo: the Smurfs.

Horta's building

Designed as a department stone in 1906, the lovely building features a swirling tiled floor, slim metal pillars, girders and grills and light filtered through a glass ceiling. As you enter, a model of Tintin's red rocket gleams against the pale stone; to the right is a small exhibition about the construction, decline and restoration of the building.

☑ **Top Tips**

▶ Don't forget to pick up the English notes at the ticket desk or you'll be all at sea.

▶ You don't have to pay an entrance fee to enjoy the central hallway or to drink a coffee (€2.20) at the attached cafe.

▶ Temporary exhibitions on the top floor show international comic-strip art.

▶ Don't miss the shop, which steers clear of merchandise and focuses on books, including *Sarkozik* – a satire on the French ex-president, plus the Smurfs, Tintin, fantasy and manga.

▶ Should you want more reading matter – albeit in French – there's a comic-book library next door.

✗ **Take a Break**

The adjoining cafe, **Brasserie Horta** (www.brasseriehorta.be; mains €14-18; ☺noon-3pm Tue-Sun), is an attractive place serving Belgian standards.

Centre Belge de la Bande Dessinée

200 m
0.1 miles

R des Cendres
R de la Blanchisserie
R du Damier
R des Sables
R du Meiboom
Blvd de Berlaimont
R du Marais
R du Persil
R des Boiteux
R Montagne aux Herbes Potagères
R d'Argent
R des Martyrs
Pl des Martyrs
R aux Choux
R Neuve
Blvd Adolphe Max
R du Finistère
R St-Michel
R de Malines
R St-Pierre
Pont-Neuf
R de la Fiancée
ARAU
Blvd Emile Jacqmain
R de l'Epargne
R du Pélican
R aux Fleurs
R du Cirque
R Van der Elst
R des Hirondelles
R de Laeken
R du Fossé aux Loups
R Léopold
R des Princes
R de la Reine
R de l'Ecuyer
R des Fripiers
Pl de la Monnaie
R de l'Evêque
R Grétry
De Brouckère
Pl de Brouckère
Blvd Anspach
R des Augustins
R des Halles
R du Marché aux Poulets
R de la Vierge Noire
R J Plateau
R Melsens
Pl Ste-Catherine
R Ste-Catherine
STE-CATHERINE
Pl du Samedi
Pl du Peuple
R du Peuplier
Marché aux Poissons
Q au Bois à Brûler
Q aux Briques
Ste-Catherine
Pl du Béguinage
R du Rouleau
R du Grand-Hospice
Q aux Pierres de Tailles
R du Canal

28
43
15
39
38
35
34

Banque National

R du Bois Sauvage

Cathédrale des Sts Michel & Gudule

R des Colonies

R Ravenstein

Pl Royale

R de Loxum

R Montagne de la Cour

R d'Arenberg

Galerie des Princes

R Cardinal Mercier

Carr de l'Europe

Blvd de l'Impératrice

R de la Montagne

R des Bouchers

Galerie du Roi

R des Dominicains

ÎLOT SACRÉ

Petite R des Bouchers

Galerie de la Reine

Pl d'Espagne

R du Marché aux Herbes

R du Marché aux Herbes

R des Harengs

R de la Colline

R du Marché aux Fromages

R des Éperonniers

R Marché aux Herbes

Impasse de la Fidélité

R de la Fourche

Grand Place

Brussels International

R de la Tête d'Or

R de l'Amigo

R des Brasseurs

R de la Violette

R des Chapeliers

R Duquesnoy

R St-Jean

Gare Centrale

Pl de l'Albertine

R de l'Infante Isabelle

R de la Madeleine

Pl de l'Albertine

Pl de la Justice

R Lebeau

SABLON

Blvd de l'Empereur

Pl St-Jean

R de l'Hôpital

R du Lombard

Pl de la Vieille Halle aux Blés

R de l'Escalier

R de Dinant

Pl de Dinant

R d'Accolay

R des Alexiens

R Auguste Orts

R van Praet

Pl de la Bourse

R de la Bourse

R Henri Maus

R des Pierres

Borgval

R de la Grande Île

R du St-Géry

Halles St Géry

R Plattesteen

R des Teinturiers

R du Midi

R du Marché au Charbon

Blvd Anspach

R du Jardin des Olives

Pl Fontainas

R des Grands Carmes

R de l'Écuyer

R de l'Étuve

R du Chêne

R Charles Buls

R des Bogards

MAROLLES

R Van Helmont

R du Poinçon

R des Tanneurs

17

12

3

41

33

31

29

27

40

36

8

9

11

26

4

37

16

13

22

18

1

6

42

5

32

23

19

7

25

30

14

20

21

24

10

2

Sights

Musée du Costume et de la Dentelle
MUSEUM

1 ⊙ Map p72, C6

Lace-making has been one of Flanders' finest crafts since the 16th century. While *kloskant* (bobbin lace) originated in Bruges, *naaldkant* (needlepoint lace) was developed in Italy but was predominantly made in Brussels. This excellent museum reveals lace's applications for under- and outerwear over the centuries, as well as displaying other luxury textiles in beautifully presented changing exhibitions. Ask for an English-language booklet. (Costume & Lace Museum; ✏02-213 44 50; www.costumeandlacemuseum.be; Rue de la Violette 12; admission €3, free with Brusselscard; ⊙10am-5pm, closed Wed; Ⓜ Gare Centrale)

Manneken Pis
MONUMENT

2 ⊙ Map p72, B7

This fountain-statue of a little boy cheerfully taking a leak is comically tiny and a perversely perfect national symbol for surreal Belgium. More often than not the statue's nakedness is largely hidden beneath a costume relevant to an anniversary, national day or local event. The Manneken Pis was designed by Jerôme Duquesnoy in 1619: this one is not the original. (Cnr Rue de l'Étuve & Rue du Chêne; Ⓜ Gare Centrale)

Jeanneke Pis
MONUMENT

3 ⊙ Map p72, C5

Why should the boys have all the fun? Squatting just off Rue des Bouchers, this pigtailed female counterpart of Manneken Pis is the work of sculptor Denis Adrien Debouvrie, who installed her here in 1985, though she's usually partly obscured by locked iron gates. Donations go to cancer research. (www.jeannekepisofficial.be; Impasse de la Fidélité; Ⓜ Gare Centrale)

Musée du Cacao et du Chocolat
MUSEUM

4 ⊙ Map p72, B6

Exhibits at Brussels' museum of cocoa and chocolate give you a quick rundown of chocolate's history in

---

☑ Top Tip

Mural-spotting

Over 40 comic-strip murals currently enliven alleys and thoroughfares throughout the old city centre, with more added every year. Most are mapped at www.brusselscomics.com/en/route_bd.cfm. Moseying past a few of these cheery murals is a great way to explore less-visited neighbourhoods. Some favourites include **Tibet & Duchateau** (Rue du Bon Secours), **Tintin** (Rue de l'Étuve), **Broussaille** (Rue du Marché au Charbon), **Peeping Policeman** (Rue Haute), **Manneken Pis Displaced** (Rue de Flandre), **Néron** (Place St-Géry), and **Le Chat** (Blvd du Midi).

Europe, as well as elucidating chocolate's anti-aging and antidepressant properties. A couple of small treats along the way include a tasting at the praline-making demonstration. Better yet are the museum's occasional one-hour praline-making courses – call for details. (☏02-514 20 48; www.mucc.be; Rue de la Tête d'Or 9; adult/concession/under 12 yr €5.50/4.50/free; ☉10am-4.30pm daily Jul & Aug, closed Mon Sep-Jun; Ⓜ Gare Centrale or 🚊 Bourse)

Fondation Jacques Brel   MUSEUM

5 ◉ Map p72, C7

Chansonnier Jacques Brel (1929–78) made his debut in 1952 at a cabaret in his native Belgium, afterwards shooting to fame in Paris where he was a contemporary of Édith Piaf. This dedicated archive centre and museum, set up by his daughter, contains hours of footage and audio recordings, plus photographs. Dedicated fans can also take the audio walking tour. (☏02-511 10 20; www.jacquesbrel.be; Place de la Vieille Halle aux Blés 11; adult/student €5/3.50, walk with audio guide €8, walk & museum €10; ☉10.30am-6pm Tue-Sat July & Aug, from noon Sept-Jun; Ⓜ Gare Centrale)

Musée de la Brasserie   MUSEUM

6 ◉ Map p72, C6

Brussels' brewery museum is authentic in that it occupies the basement of the brewers' guildhall and has some 18th-century brewing equipment. But visitors are often disappointed at its small size and the lack of real brewing

Manneken Pis

taking place (though you do get a beer at the end). If this is what you're after, head to the Cantillon Brewery's Musée Bruxellois de la Gueuze (p119). (☏02-511 49 87; www.beerparadise.be; Grand Place 10; admission €5; ☉10am-5pm daily Apr-Nov, noon-5pm Sat & Sun Dec-Mar; Ⓜ Gare Centrale or 🚊 Bourse)

Scientastic Museum   MUSEUM

7 ◉ Map p72, B5

Kids aged six and over may yet think science is fun after a couple of hours at this interactive museum (bizarrely located in the Bourse premetro station), where they can make their voice mimic a duck, 'fly' using mirrors and enjoy other sensory pursuits. One for a rainy day. (☏02-732 13 36;

www.scientastic.com; Blvd Anspach, in premetro station Bourse; adult/concession €7.90/5.30; ☉10.30am-5.30pm Mon, Tue, Thu & Fri, 2-5.30pm Wed, Sat & Sun; 🚇Bourse)

Galeries St-Hubert

SHOPPING ARCADE

8 ◎ Map p72, C6

Opened in 1847, Europe's first-ever covered shopping gallery comprises three connecting arcades beneath its lovely vaulted glass roof: Galerie du Roi, Galerie de la Reine and the smaller, perpendicular Galerie des Princes. Between them, the arcades contain a cinema, theatre, cafes and some wonderful shops selling chocolate, books and music, fashion and accessories. It was once a hangout for Victor Hugo. (www.galeries-saint-hubert.com; off Rue du Marché aux Herbes; 🚇Gare Centrale)

Eating

Café-Restaurant de l'Ogenblik

FRENCH $$$

9 🍴 Map p72, C5

It may be only stone's throw from Rue des Bouchers, but this timeless bistro with its lace curtains, resident cat, marble-topped tables and magnificent wrought-iron lamp feels a world away. They've been producing French classics here for more than 30 years, and the expertise shows. Worth the price for a special meal in the heart of town. (☎02-511 61 51; www.ogenblik.be; Galerie des

◯ Local Life

Eating Like a Local

Low-hanging awnings strung with fairy lights, oyster stands on the cobblestones and aproned waiters hustling for business cram narrow Rue des Bouchers, which intersects Galeries St-Hubert. Yes, this is tourist central, and due to the generally poor food standards locals steer clear. An exception is the classic, expensive **Aux Armes de Bruxelles** (Map p72, 5C; ☎02-511 55 98; www.aux armesdebruxelles.com; Rue des Bouchers 13; mains €6-20; ☉noon-11pm Tue-Sun; 🚇De Brouckère, 🚇Bourse).

Princes 1; mains €26-32; ☉noon-2.30pm & 7pm-midnight Mon-Sat; 🚇De Brouckère)

Le Cercle des Voyageurs

BRASSERIE $

10 🍴 Map p72, B7

Invite Phileas Fogg for coffee to this delightful bistro featuring globes, an antique-map ceiling and a travel library. If he's late, flick through old copies of *National Geographic* in your colonial leather chair. The global brasserie food is pretty good, and the free live music is fantastic: piano jazz on Tuesdays and jazz/experimental on Thursdays. Other gigs in the *cave* have a small entrance fee. (☎02-514 39 49; www.lecercledesvoyageurs.com; Rue des Grands Carmes 18; mains €9-12; ☉8am-11pm Wed-Mon; 🚇Annessens or Bourse)

Understand

Being Belgian

'Nothing works here, and still it works. That's Belgium.' Statements like this by locals sum up Belgians' acceptance of – even pride about – their country's seeming absurdity at times (the fact that it ticked along quite nicely without a federal government for months, for example). Belgians are on the whole an innovative, optimistic bunch with an easygoing outlook.

Citizens often identify themselves as Flemish (Dutch-speaking) or Walloon (French-speaking) first, and Belgian second. Moreover, Brussels is a vibrant hub of multiculturalism, whose population includes many other European nationalities as well as Moroccans, Turks and Africans (especially from the former Belgian Congo).

Religion and morals

Religion also plays a part in identity and day-to-day life, including politics and education. Roughly 75% of Belgium's population is Roman Catholic and, despite church attendance plummeting, traditions endure. Protestant communities also maintain a strong presence, and the capital has a significant Muslim population.

When it comes to moral freedom, Belgium is a world leader. Same-sex couples have been able to wed legally in Brussels since 2003, and have the same rights as heterosexual couples, including inheritance and adoption.

Language and customs

For all its quirks and contrasts, Belgium is refreshingly uncomplicated in terms of social interaction, with few pitfalls for visitors. The main issue to watch for outside of Brussels is language – the capital itself is officially bilingual but, despite being geographically in Flanders, it's predominantly French-speaking. In Bruges, if you don't want to attempt Dutch, you should speak English rather than French.

When meeting for the first time, men and women, and women and women, greet each other with three kisses on the cheek (starting on the left); after that it's usually just one kiss. Men meeting men shake hands.

Unlike in neighbouring France and the Netherlands, shopkeepers won't generally greet you when you enter their premises. This isn't unfriendliness, but rather to avoid being seen as giving the hard sell – something that's shunned by Belgians, who are unassuming by nature.

Dandoy

TEAROOM $

11 Map p72, B5

Established in 1829, Brussels' best-known *biscuiterie* – much loved by locals – has five local branches, this one with an attached tearoom. From a window it dispenses fat waffles piled with sweet toppings and artisinal ice cream. The chocolate for Dandoy's choc-dipped biscuits is handmade by Laurent Gerbaud (p96). (02-511 03 26; www.biscuiteriedandoy.be; Rue au Beurre 31; snacks from €3; 9.30am-7pm Mon-Sat, 10.30am-7pm Sun; M Gare Centrale)

Arcadi

BISTRO $

12 Map p72, D5

The jars of preserves, beautiful cakes and fruit tarts of this classic and charming bistro entice plenty of Brussels residents, as do well-priced meals like lasagne and steak, all served non-stop by courteous staff. With a nice location on the edge of the Galeries St-Hubert, this is a great spot for an indulgent creamy hot chocolate. (02-511 33 43; Rue d'Arenberg 1b; snacks from €5; 7am-11pm; M Gare Centrale)

Brasserie de la Roue d'Or

BELGIAN $$

13 Map p72, C6

Cosy in a cramped Parisian bistro sort of way, this glamorous place serves excellent if somewhat pricey Belgian food such as suckling pig, *moules* and steak. Wall murals and ceiling clouds pay homage to the city's surrealist artists. Try *crêpes flambées* or heaped profiteroles for dessert. Reservations are nearly always essential. (02-514 25 54; Rue des Chapeliers 26; mains €15-28; noon-12.30am, closed Jul; M Gare Centrale)

Kokob

ETHIOPIAN $$

14 Map p72, A7

A warmly lit Ethiopian bar/restaurant/cultural centre at the bottom of Rue des Carmes, where well-explained dishes are best shared, eaten from and with pancake-like *injera* – it's one to visit in a group rather than on your own. Traditional coffee ceremonies are held on Wednesday evening and Sunday (noon to 3pm). (02-511 19 50; www.kokob.be; Rue des Grands Carmes 10; menus from €20; 6.30pm-midnight Mon-Wed & noon-1am Thu-Sun; Annessens or Bourse)

Local Life
Where to Eat Waffles

Locals get 'real' waffles at **Mokafé** (Map p72, 5D; 02-511 78 70; Galerie du Roi; waffles from €3; 7.30am-11.30pm; M De Brouckère), an old-fashioned cafe under the glass arch of the Galeries-St Hubert. It's a little timeworn inside, but wicker chairs in the beautiful arcade provide you with a good view of passing shoppers. Note that traditional waffles have 20 squares, and are dusted with icing sugar rather than loaded with cream.

La Maison du Cygne, Grand Place

La Maison du Cygne BELGIAN $$$

16 🍴 Map p72, C6

Try for a table overlooking the Grand Place in this refined 2nd-floor restaurant where you can dine on bank-breaking but beautifully prepared Belgian classics. Service is appropriately fussy and the wine list is outstanding. Budget diners after a taste of Louis XIV grandeur should try the 1st-floor L'Ommegang bar (noon to 2pm Monday to Friday), where the *plat du jour* costs €15. (☎02-511 82 44; www.lamaisonducygne.be; Rue Charles Buls 2; mains €37-65, menu €65; ⏱lunch Mon-Fri, dinner Sun-Fri; Ⓜ Gare Centrale)

Sea Grill SEAFOOD $$$

15 🍴 Map p72, D4

It may be located in the bland atrium of the Radisson, where muzak blends with the tinkle of water features, but the food served in this Michelin-starred restaurant, created by chef Yves Mattagne and his team, is outstanding. Try the Brittany lobster, crushed and extracted in an antique solid-silver lobster press (one of only four in the world) and prepared at your table. (☎02-212 08 00; www.seagrill.be; Radisson SAS Royal Hotel Brussels, Rue du Fossé aux Loups 47; ⏱noon-2pm & 7-10pm, closed mid-July–mid-Aug; Ⓜ De Brouckère)

Drinking

À la Mort Subite PUB, BRASSERIE

17 🍷 Map p72, D5

Floor-to-ceiling square columns with brass hat-racks, massive mirrors, varnished timber panelling and leather banquettes make this a sublime place to try the namesake Mort Subite (Sudden Death) *gueuze*. If this twice-fermented beer is too sour for your taste, order a *kriek* (cherry) or *framboise* (raspberry) version. Soak it up with old-school snacks, like omelettes for under €10. (☎02-513 13 18; www.alamortsubite.com; Rue Montagne aux Herbes Potagères 7; ⏱11am-1am Mon-Sat, noon-midnight Sun; Ⓜ Gare Centrale)

Le Fonograf

BAR

18 Map p72, C7

Vibrant new 'art *café*' and bar with pared-down canteen-style decor, artfully battered furniture and monthly exhibitions of contemporary art and photography. The weekend live music events featuring jazz, funk, Balkan and South American music can be riotously good fun. Classy bar food is a bonus, as are the cocktails. (02-511 22 26; www.lefonograf.be; Rue de la Violette 32; noon-1am Sun-Thu, noon-2am Fri & Sat; Gare Centrale)

À la Bécasse

PUB

19 Map p72, B5

Hidden almost invisibly down a body-wide alley-tunnel. Long rows of tables give the Bécasse a certain Brueghelesque quality, though it's 'only' been operating since 1877. The unusual speciality is *panaché,* a jug of Timmermans lambic mixed with fruit beer or *faro* to make it more palatable. Not to everyone's taste. (www.alabecasse. com; Rue de Tabora 11; 11am-midnight, till 1am Fri & Sat; Gare Centrale)

Au Soleil

BAR

20 Map p72, A7

This old clothes shop with wooden benches, tiled floor and mirrors has been converted into a shabby-chic bar with good beats and surprisingly inexpensive drinks given its status as a favourite for posers in shades. A small kitchen serves up snacks and a few mains. (02-513 34 30; Rue du Marché au Charbon 86; 10.30am-late; Bourse)

Fontainas Bar

BAR

21 Map p72, A7

The ripped black vinyl seats, '60s tables and light fittings, and cracked tiles of this loud and ultratrendy bar provide the backdrop for locals reading newspapers by day, until the party cranks up again come nightfall. It's located on Brussels' small strip of gay-friendly establishments. (02-503 31 12; Rue du Marché au Charbon 91; 10am-late Mon-Fri, 11am-late Sat & Sun; Bourse)

Goupil le Fol

BAR

22 Map p72, C7

Overwhelming weirdness hits you as you acid-trip your way through this sensory overload of rambling passageways, ragged old sofas, floor-to-ceiling artworks and inexplicable beverages mostly based on madly fruit-flavoured wines (no beer available, which is an oddity in itself in Brussels). Belgium at its eccentric best – unmissable. Note the late opening hours. (02-511 13 96; Rue de la Violette 22; 9pm-5am; Gare Centrale)

Le Cirio

BAR

23 Map p72, B5

This sumptuous 1886 *grand café* dazzles with polished brass-work and aproned waiters, yet prices aren't exorbitant and coiffured Mesdames with small dogs still dilute the gaggles of tourists. The house speciality is a half-and-half mix of wine and champagne (remember to drop your 'h's when you order; €3.20). (Rue de la Bourse 18; ⏰10am-midnight)

Moeder Lambic Fontainas PUB

 24 Map p72, A7

At the last count they were serving 46 artisinal beers here, in a contemporary rather than old-world setting: walls are bare brick and hung with photos and the booths are backed with concrete. They serve up great quiches and cheese and meat platters. The mood is upbeat and the music loud. (☏02-503 60 68; www.moederlambic.eu; Place Fontainas 8; ⏰11am-1am Mon-Thu & Sun, 11am-2am Fri & Sat; 🚇Annessens or Bourse)

Falstaff BAR

25 Map p72, B5

The interior of this grand *café* is an astonishing festival of century-old art nouveau stained glass and fluidly carved wood designed by Horta disciple Houbion. It is rather on the overpriced and touristy side, but the architecture means that it is worth at least one drink; if you decide to stay, you'll find a wide range of meals available. (Rue Henri Maus 17; ⏰10am-1am; 🚇Bourse)

Entertainment

Music Village JAZZ

26 Map p72, B6

This polished 100-seat jazz venue housed in two 17th-century buildings has dinner (not compulsory) available from 7pm and concerts starting at 8.30pm, or 9pm on weekends. They feature everything from Cuban to Polish to Chilean jazz as well as New Orleans brass and some experimental music. Table seating; bookings advised. (☏02-513 1345; www.themusic village.com; Rue des Pierres 50; cover €7.50-20; ⏰from 7.30pm Wed-Sat; 🚇Bourse)

☑ Top Tip

Wrong Coffee

Belgium may brew beer brilliantly, but when it comes to coffee, it's no Italy. Cappuccino froth is frequently made from artificial whipped cream, and generally the closest thing you'll get to a latte is a *koffie verkeerd* (or *lait Russe* 'Russian milk' in French; the Dutch name literally translates as 'wrong coffee' since it has more milk than coffee). If you simply ask for 'coffee', you'll be brought a regular-size cup of black coffee (invariably called an espresso, regardless of the machinery used) with a tub of long-life milk and, by way of compensation, a small chocolate or biscuit.

Théâtre Royal de Toone
PUPPET THEATRE

27 ⭐ Map p72, C5

Eight generations of the Toone family have staged classic puppet productions in the Bruxellois dialect at this endearing marionette theatre, a highlight of any visit to Brussels. Shows are aimed at adults, but kids love them too. The irresistibly quaint and cosy timber-framed bar serves beers and basic snacks (noon till midnight). (☎02-511 71 37; www.toone.be; Petite Rue des Bouchers 21; adult/child €10/7; ⏱typically 8.30pm Thu & 4pm Sat, see website; Ⓜ Gare Centrale)

Art Base
LIVE MUSIC

28 ⭐ Map p72, E3

A plain but appealing small venue and gallery space opposite the cartoon museum, with a serious and eclectic program of live music: tango, Greek, flamenco and Latin. Lovers of Indian classical music should look out for the Sunday night gigs. Also open sporadically during the day as an art gallery; gigs are generally Thusday to Sunday. (☎02-217 29 20; www.art-base.be; rue des Sables 29; Ⓜ Rogier)

Actor's Studio
CINEMA

29 ⭐ Map p72, C5

This intimate and tucked away three-screen cinema, a little hard to locate just off touristy Le Petite Rue des Bouchers, shows arthouse flicks as well as some mainstream reruns, and has a tiny bar. Try to catch a movie here – it's one of the city's indie treasures and the tickets are cheaper than in the big movie houses. (☎02-512 16 96; Petite Rue des Bouchers 16; Ⓡ Bourse)

AB
LIVE MUSIC

30 ⭐ Map p72, A6

The AB's two auditoriums are favourite venues for mid-level international rock bands and acts such as Jules Holland and Madeleine Peyroux, plus plenty of home-grown talent. The ticket office is located on Rue des Pierres. There's a good on-site bar/restaurant that opens at 6pm (bookings essential). (Ancienne Belgique; ☎02-548 24 00; www.abconcerts.be; Blvd Anspach 110; Ⓡ Bourse)

Cinéma Galeries
CINEMA

31 ⭐ Map p72, C5

Inside the graceful glassed-over Galeries St-Hubert, this art deco beauty concentrates on foreign and arthouse films. Forget the multiplexes and try an authentic Brussels movie experience. (☎02-514 74 98; www.arenberg.be; Galerie de la Reine 26, Galeries St-Hubert; Ⓜ Gare Centrale)

Le You
CLUB

32 ⭐ Map p72, C7

Somewhat mainstream, but in a sterling location just off the Grand Place, this vast club has a labyrinth of dance floors and chill-out rooms, and gay tea dances on Sundays (www.leyougayteadance.be). (☎02-639 14 00;

www.leyou.be; Rue Duquesnoy 18; admission Thu-Sat €10, Sun €6; ⏱11pm-5am Thu, 11.30am-6am Fri & Sat, 8pm-2am Sun; Ⓜ Gare Centrale)

Théâtre du Vaudeville   THEATRE

33 ⭐ Map p72, D6

Cabarets, concerts and various theatre productions take place at this old

---

Q Local Life

Jazz in Brussels

Jazz has a special place in Belgium, the home of Adolphe Sax (inventor of the saxophone), gypsy guitar king Django Reinhardt and octogenarian harmonica whiz Toots Thielemans, who is still going strong as a performer. Along with Music Village (p81), other long established and much-loved venues include the **Jazz Station** (☎02-733 13 78; http://jazzstation.be; Chaussée de Louvain 193a; ⏱exhibitions 11am-7pm Wed-Sat, concerts 6pm Sat & 8.30pm some weeknights) on rue Antoine Dansaert, **L'Archiduc** (Map p72, A4; ☎02-512 06 52; www.archiduc. net; Rue Antoine Dansaert 6; beer/wine/cocktails €2.70/3.60/8; ⏱4pm-late) and **Sounds** (☎02-512 92 50; www. soundsjazzclub.be; Rue de la Tulipe 28; ⏱8pm-4am Mon-Sat) in Ixelles. The **Brussels Jazz Marathon** (www. brusselsjazzmarathon.be) is held in venues across the city in May, while the **Skoda Jazz Festival** (www. skodajazz.be) goes country-wide in October and November.

---

theatre within the Galeries St-Hubert. Program leaflets are available in the foyer inside the arcade. (☎02-512 57 45; Galerie de la Reine 13-15, Galeries St-Hubert; Ⓜ Gare Centrale)

Théâtre Royal de la Monnaie/Koninklijke Muntschouwburg   OPERA, DANCE

34 ⭐ Map p72, C4

The theatre occupies a central role in the city's history: Belgium was born when an opera staged at this venue inspired the 1830 revolution (see p97). Nowadays it primarily shows contemporary dance, as well as classic and new operas. (☎02-229 13 72; Place de la Monnaie; Ⓜ De Brouckère)

Théâtre National   THEATRE

35 ⭐ Map p72, C1

By virtue of being a bilingual city, the Belgian capital has not one but two national theatres. This new glass-fronted theatre is the Francophone counterpart to the Flemish Koninklijke Vlaamse Schouwburg. (☎02-203 41 55; www.theatrenational.be; Blvd Émile Jacqmain 111-115; Ⓜ Gare Centrale)

Shopping

Boutique Tintin   COMICS

36 🛍 Map p72, C6

No prizes for guessing the star of this little comic shop just off the Grand Place, which stocks albums galore and cute merchandise. For more Tintin gear and other cartoon classics, head to the Centre Belge de la Bande Dessinée (p70). (📞02-514 51 52; Rue de la Colline 13; ⏰10am-6pm Mon-Sat, 11am-5pm Sun; 🚻; Ⓜ Gare Centrale)

Catherine
CHEESE

37 🔒 Map p72, B6

A traditional and welcoming grocery in the heart of town, specialising in artisinal cheeses, several of them organic. You'll also find cured meats and condiments – all the perfect basis for a simple supper if you're self-catering. (📞02-512 75 64; Rue du Midi 23; ⏰9am-6pm Mon-Sat; 🚌 Bourse)

Passage du Nord
SHOPPING ARCADE

38 🔒 Map p72, C3

Passage du Nord's array of quality boutiques makes this vaulted glass arcade a good spot to escape the rain: there's a cute oyster bar, a pharmacy and a branch of long-established Neuhaus chocolates. (off Rue Neuve; Ⓜ De Brouckère)

Sterling Books
BOOKS

39 🔒 Map p72, D4

There's a fantastic selection of travel guides on the 1st floor of this friendly English-language bookshop, plus a good range of history and art books that you're welcome to browse at leisure. Put your feet up on the comfy sofas: there's also a kids' play area.

(📞02-223 62 23; www.sterlingbooks.be; Rue du Fossé aux Loups 38; ⏰10am-7pm Mon-Sat, noon-6.30pm Sun; Ⓜ De Brouckère)

De Biertempel
BEER

40 🔒 Map p72, C5

As its name states, this shop is a temple to beer, stocking upwards of 700 brews along with matching glasses and other booze-related merchandise. For more ordinary beers and for bulk puchases, make like the locals and go to the supermarket. (📞02-502 19 06; www.biertempel.be; Rue du Marché aux Herbes 56b; ⏰9.30am-7pm; 🚌 Bourse)

Delvaux
ACCESSORIES

41 🔒 Map p72, D5

Survey the gleaming and brightly coloured handbags at Belgium's own Delvaux, established in 1829 and apparently the world's oldest luxury leather goods company. Quality comes at a high price though: be prepared to part with around €950 for a bag. (📞02-512 71 98; www.delvaux.be; Galerie de la Reine 31; ⏰10am-6.30pm Mon-Sat; Ⓜ Gare Centrale)

Neuhaus
CHOCOLATE

Belgium's original *chocolatier* was established in this gorgeous arched arcade (see **41** 🔒 Map p72, D5) in 1857 by the inventor of the praline and remains virtually unchanged since. It's a feast for both the eyes and the tastebuds: this stunning flagship shop has stained-glass windows and sump-

Neuhaus window display

tuous displays. (☎02-512 63 59; www.neuhaus.be; Galerie de la Reine 25; chocolate per kg €52; ⏱10am-8pm Mon-Sat, 10am-7pm Sun; Ⓜ Gare Centrale)

Planète Chocolat
CHOCOLATE

42 🔒 Map p72, B6

You can catch praline-making demonstrations every Saturday and Sunday at 4pm (€7) at this experimental chocolatier famed for its chocolate floral 'bouquets' and other innovative shapes such as chessboards and cockerels. (☎02-511 07 55; www.planetechocolat.be; Rue du Lombard 24; per kg €50; ⏱11am-6pm Mon & Sun, 10.30am-6.30pm Tue-Sat; 🚊 Bourse)

City 2
SHOPPING MALL

43 🔒 Map p72, E1

This bland but handy modern shopping mall has all the usual chain-store suspects, plus a branch of the Carrefour supermarket which is good for cheap beer buys and self-caterers. In the mall's basement you'll find a post office, and a better-than-average food court – try **Ganesh** for fantastic Indian samosas, curries and naan breads. (Rue Neuve 123; Ⓜ Rogier)

Explore

Royal Quarter Museums

The majestic Royal Quarter takes in the Palais Royal, the Palais de Justice, and the Mont des Arts, where Brussels' premier museums are housed a few steps from each other. Antique shops, tearooms and chocolate boutiques – frequented by fur-coated *Mesdames* and coiffed pooches – cluster around the Place du Grand Sablon, while graceful churches and the elegant Parc de Bruxelles add to the area's rarefied air.

The Sights in a Day

☀ Start your day at the **Musées Royaux des Beaux-Arts** (p88), seeing the work of the Flemish Primitives, Brueghel's *Fall of Icarus* and the adjoining **Magritte Museum** (p89). Head to one of the *cafés* on the Place du Grand Sablon for lunch, or pick up a picnic at **Clare Fontaine** (p100) and enjoy it on the Place du Petit Sablon.

☀ Be sure to peek into the **Église Notre Dame du Sablon** (p94) while you're here. Then make a beeline for the **Musée des Instruments de Musique** (p90), housed in the art nouveau Old England Building. Take a tea break in the rooftop cafe, or head downhill for **Laurent Gerbaud's** (p96) famous chocolates and a cuppa. To find out more about Belgium's history, check out the **Musée BELvue** (p95), located in an elegant former palace.

☽ For dinner, enjoy brasserie food at the charming **Le Perroquet** (p99) or, for something more upmarket, be sure to book ahead for **Les Brigittines** (p96). Later, take in a high-brow concert at **BOZAR** (p100), or enjoy the live piano accompaniment of a silent classic at the **Cinematek** (p100).

👁 Top Sights

Musées Royaux des Beaux-Arts (p88)

Musée des Instruments de Musique (p90)

💗 Best of Brussels

Best Shops for Chocolate
Mary (p101)

Pierre Marcolini (p101)

Laurent Gerbaud (p96)

Best Speciality Museums
Musée des Instruments de Musique (p90)

Magritte Museum (p89)

Musée BELvue (p95)

Best Churches
Église Notre-Dame du Sablon (p94)

Cathédrale des Sts-Michel & Gudule (p94)

Église Notre-Dame de la Chapelle (p94)

Getting There

M **Metro** stops Louise and Porte de Namur are the handiest for the Place du Sablon; Gare Central is best for Mont des Arts.

🚊 **Premetro** 92, 93 and 94 pass through the district.

Top Sights
Musées Royaux des Beaux-Arts

The prestigious Royal Museums of Fine Arts incorporate both the **Musée d'Art Ancien** (ancient art) and the **Musée d'Art Moderne** (modern art). Among the many highlights are collections of the Flemish Primitives, the Brueghels (especially Pieter the Elder) and Rubens in the Musée d'Art Ancien; and works by surrealist Paul Delvaux and fauvist Rik Wouters in the subterranean Musée d'Art Moderne. The complex also celebrates the country's favourite surrealist son in the purpose-built **Musée René Magritte**.

Map p92, C5

☏ 02-508 32 11

www.fine-arts-museum.be

Rue de la Régence 3

adult/student €8/5; €13 if combined with Magritte Museum

🕑 10am-5pm Tue-Sun

Ⓜ Gare Centrale or Parc

Interior of the Musées Royaux des Beaux-Arts

Don't Miss

The Flemish Primitives

The work of these 15th-century masters is wonderfully represented here: look out for Rogier Van der Weyden's *Pietà* with its hallucinatory dawn sky; Dieric Bouts' dramatic tableau, *The Justice of the Emperor Otto*; Hans Memling's refined portraits; and the richly textured *Madonna With Saints* by the Master of the Legend of St Lucy.

The Brueghels

While Pieter the Elder was the greatest of this family of artists, his sons' work echoes his humorous and tender scenes, featuring a wealth of lively rustic detail. The most famous example is the *Fall of Icarus*, where the hero's legs disappearing into the waves are overshadowed by the figure of an unconcerned ploughman and a jaunty ship.

Rubens and his followers

Inspired by the Renaissance artists, Antwerp painter Peter Paul Rubens specialised in fleshy religious works, of which there are several colossal examples here. But his lesser-known works, such as his *Studies of a Negro's Head,* show he was also a master of psychological portraiture. In this section, look out too for Anthony van Dyck's contemplative human studies, Cornelius de Vos' charming family portrait, and works by Rembrandt and Frans Hals.

The Magritte Museum

The adjoining **Magritte Museum** (www.musee -magritte-museum.be; Place Royale; adult/under 26yr/ BrusselsCard €8/2/free; ⏰10am-5pm Tue-Sun) offers a chronological exploration of the artist's work, including surreal and playful photos and films.

☑ Top Tips

▶ On the first Wednesday of the month, this and many other Brussels museums are free from 1pm. Don't plan to see any Brussels museum on a Monday – they'll be firmly closed.

▶ Consider visiting the Magritte Museum separately as it merits at least two hours – you can buy a joint ticket and return another day.

▶ The museum also hosts acclaimed temporary exhibitions, for which there's an extra charge.

▶ Check out the small sculpture garden, to the left as you face the building.

✕ Take a Break

The museum cafe is a pricey but pleasant spot serving sandwiches, salads and cakes, with a terrace punctuated with statues overlooking the rooftops (open the same hours as the museum).

Top Sights
Musée des Instruments de Musique

This groundbreaking museum is a celebration of music in all its forms, as well as a repository for more than 2000 historic instruments. The emphasis is very much on listening, with auditory experiences around every corner, from arcane shepherds' bagpipes to Chinese carillons to harpsichords. The cumulative effect is very moving, mapping human experience through the infinite variety of our music. The superb setting, in the elongated and ornate art nouveau Old England Building, enhances an unusual and unmissable museum experience.

Map p92, C4

☎02-545 01 30

www.mim.fgov.be

Rue Montagne de la Cour 2

adult/concession €5/4

🕑9.30am-5pm Tue-Fri, 10am-5pm Sat & Sun

Ⓜ Gare Centrale or Parc

Display at the Musée des Instruments de Musique

Don't Miss

Sound Lab

The exhibits in this dimly lit gallery are numbered, with each number corresponding to a point on the soundtrack you hear via headphones. Sounds range from a 16th-century church bell chiming midnight to a 19th-century bird organ and 20th-century Hammond organ blues. Amongst the artefacts is a barrel organ with wooden figures which, when animated, enact various grisly teeth-pulling operations.

Traditional Instruments

This gallery contains every instrument you've ever heard of, and then some. You can appreciate the aesthetic qualities of actual instruments from around the world as well as – via the headphones – musical mastery, from the intricacies of the Indian sitar to the otherworldly wail of Tibetan horns to Congolese drums and harps. One of the weirdest sights and sounds is the Mardi Gras bear mask from Limbourg in Belgium, sitting alongside rough-hewn instruments and with accompanying primitive chants.

Western Art Music

A precious collection of western wind, string and keyboard instruments. The early variations on pianos, painted with delicate flowers and pastoral scenes, are amongst the most attractive items on display; look out too for the huge serpent-headed bassoons. As with the other galleries, plug in your headphones to listen as well as look.

The Old England Building

The art nouveau Old England building, formerly a department store built in 1899 by Paul Saintenoy, is much of a highlight as the museum itself. It includes a panoramic rooftop cafe and terrace.

☑ Top Tips

▶ Headphones are essential for a visit, but don't worry if you don't speak French or Flemish – all you'll hear is music.

▶ There is no labelling in English, so collect a handout at the entrance to each gallery.

▶ The museum shop has a great collection of CDs: it closes for an hour from 12.30pm.

▶ To see the building but not the museum, take the lift to the top floor and make your way back down via the stairs.

▶ There are regular concerts in the museum's recital hall: check the What's On section of the website.

✗ Take a Break

Head to the top floor for spectacular views framed by wrought-iron curlicues at **Cafétéria du Mim** (☎ 02-502 95 08; www.restomim.com; Rue Montagne de la Cour 2; meals €12-16; ☺10am-4.30pm, closed Mon).

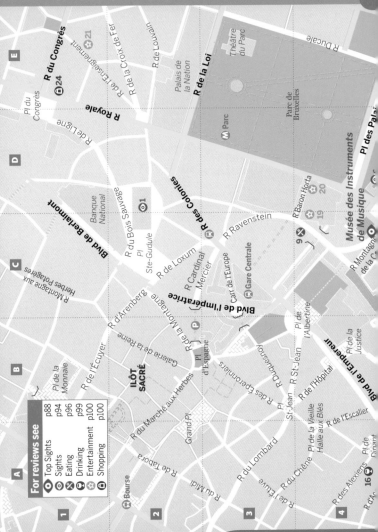

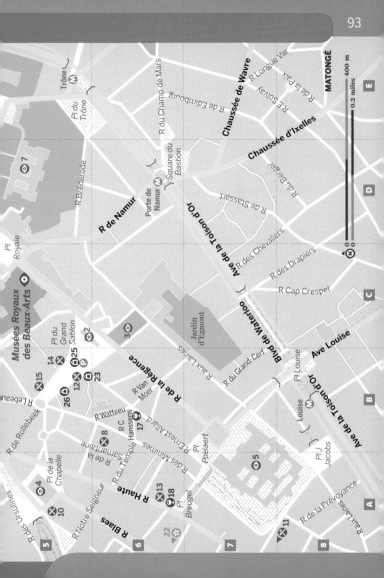

MATONGÉ

400 m
0.2 miles

Trône Ⓜ
Pl du Trône
R du Champ de Mars
R de Edimbourg
Chaussée de Wavre
R Longue Vie
R E Solvy
R de la Paix

Chaussée d'Ixelles

R du Bélier
R de Stassart

Square du Bastion

Porte de Namur Ⓜ

R de Namur

R Bréderode

⊙ 7

Pt Royale

Musées Royaux des Beaux-Arts ⊙

Ave de la Toison d'Or

R des Chevaliers

R des Drapiers

R Cap Crespel

Ⓝ

E

D

C

Pl du Grand Sablon
⊙ 2

⊙ 3

Jardin d'Egmont

Blvd de Waterloo

Ave Louise

R aux Laines

R du Grand Cerf

14 ✕
✕ 15
☒ 25 Ⓟ
12 ✕ Ⓘ
23 ☒
26 ☒

R Lebeau

R de Rollebeek

R de la Régence

R Van Moer

R Watteeu
R des Minimes

R C
E Allard
17 ☒

Pl Poelaert

Pl Louise

Louise Ⓜ

Ave de la Toison d'Or

Pl J Jacobs

B

R de la Samaritaine
R du Temple Hanssens
8 ✕

R de Rollebeek

Pl de la Chapelle
⊙ 4
✕ 10

R des Ursulines

R Blaes

R Notre Seigneur

R Haute

13 ✕
18 ⊙
Pl Breugel

22 ✡

⊙ 5

✕ 11
R aux Laines
R de la Prévoyance

5

6

7

8

A

Sights

Cathédrale des Sts-Michel & Gudule
CHURCH

1 ◉ Map p92, D2

Host to coronations and royal weddings, Brussels' grand, twin-towered cathedral bears at least a passing resemblance to Paris' Notre Dame. Begun in 1226, the construction took some 300 years. Stained-glass windows flood the soaring nave with light, while column-saints brandish gilded tools. An enormous wooden pulpit, sculpted by Antwerp artist Hendrik Verbruggen, sees Adam and Eve driven out of Eden by fearsome skeletons. (www.cathedralestmichel.be; Place Sainte-Gudule; admission free/treasury €2.50; ☉cathedral 7am-6pm Mon-Fri, 8.30am-6pm Sat, 2pm-6pm Sun; treasury 10am-12.30pm & 2-5pm Mon-Fri, till 3pm Sat, 2-5pm Sun; Ⓜ Gare Centrale)

Église Notre-Dame du Sablon
CHURCH

2 ◉ Map p92, C5

The Sablon's flamboyantly Gothic church started life in 1304 as the archers' guild chapel. A century later, however, it was massively enlarged to accommodate pilgrims visiting its Madonna statue, stolen from a church in Antwerp in 1348 by a vision-motivated couple in a rowing boat. It has long since gone, but a boat behind the pulpit commemorates the curious affair. (Rue de la Régence; ☉9am-6pm Mon-Fri, 10am-6pm Sat & Sun; Ⓜ Porte de Namur)

Place du Petit Sablon
PARK

3 ◉ Map p92, C6

About 200m uphill from Place du Grand Sablon, this charming little garden is ringed by 48 lively bronze statuettes representing the medieval guilds. Standing huddled on a fountain plinth like two actors from a Shakespearean drama are Counts Egmont and Hoorn, popular city leaders who were beheaded on the Grand Place in 1568 for defying Spanish rule. (Ⓜ Porte de Namur)

Église Notre-Dame de la Chapelle
CHURCH

4 ◉ Map p92, A5

Brussels' oldest surviving church now curiously incorporates the decapitated

---

☑ Top Tip

Brussels Greeters

A great way of exploring a specific area or indulging in a passion for anything from gueuze beers to Belgian politics, is to contact Brussels Greeters (www.brussels.greeters.be) two weeks before your trip. You fill in a simple online form and the coordinator sets you up with a local who will take you to relevant sights in the city, usually with stops for coffee and lunch along the way (trips take 2-4 hours). There is no charge for the service, and tips are not accepted.

Place du Petit Sablon

tower of the 1134 original as the central section of a larger Gothic edifice. Behind the palm-tree pulpit, look on the wall above a carved confessional to find a small memorial to 'Petro Brevgello', ie Pieter Brueghel the Elder, who once lived in the nearby Marolles. (Place de la Chapelle; admission free, pamphlet €3; ⊙9am-7pm Jun-Sep, 9am-6pm Oct-May)

Palais de Justice   HISTORIC BUILDING

5 ◉ Map p92, A7

This colossal legal complex was the world's biggest building when constructed (1866–83). Designed to evoke an Egyptian temple, it was situated on the hill dominating the working-class Marolles as an intimidating symbol of law and order. When architect Joseph Poelaert went insane and died during construction, legend suggested he'd been struck down by the witchcraft of evicted Marolles residents. (☎02-508 64 10; Place Poelaert; admission free; ⊙8am-5pm Mon-Fri; Ⓜ Louise)

Musée BELvue   MUSEUM

6 ◉ Map p92, D4

Take a chronological audio tour through the airy stuccoed interior of this former royal residence to explore the story of Belgium's history from independence to today, brought to life by exhibits and film footage. Amongst the artefacts is the jacket worn by Albert I when he died in a climbing accident in 1934. In summer, the restaurant has tables in the charming garden. (📞07-022 04 92; www.belvue.be; Place des Palais 7; adult/concession €5/4; 🕙10am-5pm Tue-Fri, till 6pm Sat & Sun; 🅼Parc)

Palais Royal   PALACE

7 ◉ Map p92, D5

These days Belgium's royal family live at Laeken but this 19th-century palace, only open in summer, remains their 'official' residence. The unlikely decor includes a ceiling clad with the wings of 1.4 million Thai jewel beetles. You'll also see contemporary royal portraits. (📞02-551 20 20; www.monarchy.be; Place des Palais; admission free; 🕙10.30am-4.30pm Tue-Sun late Jul-early Sep; 🅼Parc)

Eating

Soul Food   ORGANIC $$

8 🍴 Map p92, B6

With an intimate informal atmosphere, tiled floors and homey decor, Soul Food is a distinctly different dinner stop on the edge of the Marolles, ideal if Belgian food is beginning to weigh you down. The fusion food is organic and additive-free, and steers clear of butter and cream in favour of interesting oils, grains and seeds. Advance booking required (📞02-513 52 13; www.soulresto.com; Rue de la Samaritaine 20; mains €15-22; 🕙7-10pm Wed-Sun; 🖉; 🅼Louise)

Laurent Gerbaud   CHOCOLATE $

9 🍴 Map p92, C4

A bright and welcoming cafe with big picture windows that's perfect for lunch or a coffee. Don't leave without trying the wonderful chocolates, which count as healthy eating in the world of Belgian chocs – they have no alcohol, additives or added sugar. Friendly owner Laurent also runs chocolate tasting and making sessions. (📞02-511 16 02; www.chocolatsgerbaud.be; Rue Ravenstein 2; 🕙8am-7.30pm)

Les Brigittines   FRENCH, BELGIAN $$$

10 🍴 Map p92, A5

Grown-up and expensive eating in a muted belle époque dining room. Les Brigittines dishes up traditional

---

☑️ Top Tip

Mussels in Brussels

Steaming cast-iron pots of mussels (*mosselen* in Dutch, *moules* in French) appear on restaurant tables everywhere. They're traditionally cooked in white wine, with variations like *à la Provençal* (with tomato) and *à la bière* (in beer and cream), and are accompanied by fries. Mussels were previously only eaten during months with an 'r' in their name, to be assured of their freshness, but modern cultivation techniques now mean mussels from July onwards are considered OK. Never eat any that haven't opened properly once they've been cooked.

Understand

Belgian Independence and the Congo

Belgium has a long history of colonisation, beginning in the mid-16th century when Brussels was proclaimed capital of the Spanish Netherlands. French attempts to dominate Europe meant many wars were fought in this buffer region; fighting came to a head during the War of Spanish Succession (1701–13), which saw the Spanish Netherlands handed to the Austrians. The Austrian Hapsburgs ruled for 81 years, until the French reclaimed the region in 1794. When, in 1815, Napoleon Bonaparte was defeated at the Battle of Waterloo near Brussels, the United Kingdom of the Netherlands, incorporating the Netherlands, Belgium and Luxembourg, was created.

Revolution

Belgium finally achieved independence via an unlikely revolution of opera-goers. The opera – staged in Brussels in August 1830 and concerning Naples' uprising against the Spanish – inspired the bourgeois audience to join the workers who were demonstrating outside against the Dutch rulers. Together, opera-goers and workers stormed the town hall, and a new nation was created.

Coronation and Nationalism

At the Conference of London in January 1831, Belgium was officially declared a neutral state and Léopold of Saxe-Coburg Gotha became King Léopold I of Belgium; the country now celebrates his coronation on 21 July as its National Day holiday. The ensuing years saw the beginnings of Flemish nationalism, with growing tension between Dutch and French speakers eventually leading to the language partition in 1898.

The Belgian Congo

Léopold II came to the throne in 1865, and in 1885 he personally acquired a huge slice of central Africa – an area 70 times larger than Belgium. Over the following 25 years, five to eight million Congolese died due to legally permitted atrocities committed in the rubber plantations. In 1908, in the face of mounting international pressure, the king was compelled to cede possession of the Congo to the Belgian state, which continued to hold the territory until 1960. For more on the Belgian Congo, a good place to start is *King Leopold's Ghost* by Adam Hochschild.

French and Belgian food: the classic (and very meaty) dishes include veal cheek, pigs' trotters and steak tartare. Staff are knowledgeable about local beer and artisanal wines, and can advise on pairing your food with great booze. (02-512 68 91; www.lesbrigittines. com; Place de la Chapelle 5; mains €16-24; noon-2.30pm & 7pm-10.30pm Mon-Fri, noon-2.30pm & 7pm-11pm Sat; Louise)

Restobières   BELGIAN $$

11 ✖️ Map p92, A8

Beer-based twists on typical Belgian meals served in a delightful if slightly cramped restaurant. The walls are plastered with bottles, grinders and countless antique souvenir biscuit tins featuring Belgian royalty. Try the *carbonnade* (beef stew), or *lapin aux pruneaux* (braised rabbit with prunes). (02-502 72 51; www.restobieres. eu; Rue des Renards 9; mains €12-22, menus €18-38; noon-3pm Tue-Sat, 6.30pm-11pm Thu-Sat, 4pm-11pm Sun)

Lola   BRASSERIE $$

12 ✖️ Map p92, B5

Streamlined contemporary brasserie right on Brussels' prettiest square. The menu is a combination of seasonal French and Italian (like rack of lamb with thyme and onion confit and dauphinois potatoes), but it's the effervescent conversations of the well-heeled clientele bouncing off the stone and wood surfaces that really give this place its buzz. (02-514 24 60; Place du Grand Sablon 33; mains €14-18; noon-3pm & 6.30-11.30pm Mon-Fri, noon-11.30pm Sat & Sun; Porte de Namur)

Easy Tempo   PIZZA $

13 ✖️ Map p92, A6

Suave pizza joint in an old *boulangerie* (bakery) with a gorgeous ceramic-tiled wall that's now a protected monument. The ultrafriendly crew skims along the counter, topping pizzas with marinated aubergine, sun-dried tomatoes and artichokes. (02-513 54 40; Rue Haute 146; pizzas from €8; lunch Tue-Sun, dinner Tue-Sat; Louise)

Wittamer pâtisserie

part of the 1910-established Wittamer family's chocolate business, and a venerable Sablon tradition. You can buy the Wittamer family's chocolates at their nearby boutique at no 6. (📞02-512 37 42; www.wittamer.com; Place du Grand Sablon 12-13; snacks from €8; ⏰10am-6pm Tue-Fri, 9am-6pm Sat & Sun; Ⓜ Porte de Namur)

Drinking

La Fleur en Papier Doré CAFÉ

16 🍺 Map p92, A4

The nicotine-stained walls of this tiny *café*, adored by artists and locals, are covered with writings, art and scribbles by Magritte and his surrealist pals, some of which were reputedly traded for free drinks.'*Ceci n'est pas un musée*', quips a sign on the door reminding visitors to buy a drink and not just look around. (www.goudblomme keinpapier.be; Rue des Alexiens 53; ⏰11am-midnight Tue-Sat, 11am-7pm Sun)

Le Perroquet BAR

17 🍺 Map p92, B6

Perfect for a drink, but also good for a simple bite (salads and variations on *croques monsieurs*), this art nouveau *café* with its stained glass, marble tables and timber panelling is an atmospheric, inexpensive stop in an area that's light on such places. Popular with expats. (Rue Watteeu 31; ⏰noon-1am; Ⓜ Porte de Namur)

Le Village de la Bande Dessinée CAFE $$

14 🍴 Map p92, B5

Cartoon-themed burgers, Belgian specialities, bagels, salads and milkshakes all designed to appeal to kids. Red and white gingham tablecloths add to the jolly vibe, but there's also a serious collection of cartoons and memorabilia in the bookshop, and a gallery hung with original Hergé drawings. (📞02-523 13 23; Place du Grand Sablon 8; snacks from €6; Ⓜ Porte de Namur)

Wittamer CAFE

15 🍴 Map p92, B5

Framed by candy-pink awnings, this tempting pâtisserie and tearoom are

Brasserie Ploegmans
BRASSERIE

18 Map p92, A6

Old-fashioned mirror-panelled seats and 1927 chequerboard flooring make this a classic local hostelry that's also well regarded for its typical Bruxellois meals. (www.ploegmans.be; Rue Haute 148; ☺noon-2.30pm Tue-Fri & 6pm-10pm Tue-Sat, closed Aug; MLouise)

Entertainment

BOZAR
LIVE MUSIC

19 Map p92, C4

This celebrated classical-music venue is home to the National Orchestra and Philharmonic Society. From the outside, the Horta-designed 1928 art deco building is unobtrusive, but its Henri Le Bœuf Hall is considered to be one of the five best in the world for acoustic quality. (www.bozar.be; Palais des Beaux-Arts, Rue Ravenstein 23; MGare Centrale)

> ☑ Top Tip
> **Discount Tickets**
> If you're planning a night out, your first stop should be the tourist office on Rue Royale 2 (p157). Here a ticket desk (12.30pm to 5.30pm) sells heavily discounted tickets for concerts, theatre and cinema, from the grand BOZAR to tucked-away arthouse movie theatres.

Cinematek
CINEMA

20 Map p92, D4

In a wing of the BOZAR cultural centre, the modern and stylish Cinematek includes a little museum where you can browse through archives and memorabilia. The real highlight, though, is the program of silent films screened nearly every day at the cinema, with live piano accompaniment. There's also an impressive program of arthouse films. (☎02-507 83 70; www.cinematheque.be; Rue Baron Horta 9; MGare Centrale)

Cirque Royal
THEATRE

21 Map p92, E1

This converted indoor circus is now a venue for dance, operetta, classical and contemporary music. (☎02 218 20 15; www.cirque-royal.org; Rue de l'Enseignement 81; MMadou)

Théâtre Les Tanneurs
THEATRE

22 Map p92, A6

Sitting on the edge of the Marolles, this theatre is known for dynamic drama and dance. (☎02-512 17 84; www.lestanneurs.be; Rue des Tanneurs 75; MLouise)

Shopping

Clare Fontaine
DELI

23 Map p92, B5

Just off Place du Sablon, this is a tiny but atmospheric tile-floored *épicerie*,

Local Life
Recyclart

A glimpse into 'alternative' Brussels, this graffitied 'arts laboratory' in the old Chapelle station along Rue des Ursulines revitalised what was once an industrial wasteland. **Recyclart** (☏02-502 57 34; www. recyclart.be; Rue des Ursulines 25; ☎; ⓜAnneessens) now hosts cutting-edge gigs, parties with DJs, art installations and theatre productions, and has a daytime cafe; above is a skate park.

fragrant with spices and home-cooked dishes – there's a small kitchen at the back. Perfect for a nutritious and filling take-out sandwich or quiche, or you can stock up on oils, wine and boxes of *pain d'épices* (spiced biscuits). (☏02-512 24 10; Rue Ernest Allard 3; ⓜPorte de Namur)

Mary   CHOCOLATE

24 🔒 Map p92, E1

Established in 1919, and supplying Belgium's royal family with chocolates since 1942, Mary's is the grande dame of praline makers. All 70-plus varieties of all-natural chocolate (including scrumptious coffee creams) are cre-

ated entirely by hand. (☏02-217 45 00; www.marychoc.be; Rue Royale 73; per kg €56; ⊙10am-7pm Mon-Sat; ⓜMadou)

Sablon Antiques
Market   ANTIQUES MARKET

25 🔒 Map p92, B5

Over 100 vendors fill this stately square on weekends, selling crockery, crystal, jewellery, furniture, 18th-century Breton Faïence (pottery) and other relics of bygone eras. Prices generally reflect the high quality of goods for sale. (www.sablonantiques market.com; Place du Grand Sablon; ⊙9am-6pm Sat, 9am-2pm Sun; ⓜPorte de Namur)

Pierre Marcolini   CHOCOLATE

26 🔒 Map p92, B5

Brussels-born Marcolini is the wunderkind of Belgian chocolate-makers. His pralines include melt-in-your-mouth ganaches (cream-filled chocolate) made from exotic teas, as well as other innovations such as quirky bunny-eared Easter eggs. Choose at the glass counter then head to the back room to pick up your order. There are more designer offerings upstairs. (☏02-512 43 14; www.marcolini. be; per kg €70; ⊙10am-7pm Sun-Thu, 10am-6pm Fri & Sat; ⓜPorte de Namur)

Explore

Parc du Cinquantenaire & EU Quarter

The EU area doesn't have the best reputation, with its bland office blocks and thundering traffic. But there are plenty of sights to entice visitors, notably the museums grouped around leafy Parc du Cinquantenaire. Some fine early 20th-century houses fringe Place Marie-Louise and – of course – this is the heart of European politics, whether you see that as an enticement or an obstacle.

The Sights in a Day

☼ Have a stroll round Parc Léopold, and, if you're interested in EU politics, drop into the **EU Parliament** (p109) for their 10am tour. Otherwise, walk with the dinosaurs at the spectacular **Musée des Sciences Naturelles** (p109). Head to the **Parc du Cinquantenaire** (p104), and take in a lofty view of the district from the arcade accessed via the military museum. Detour out of the park to see the glinting facade of the art nouveau **Maison Cauchie** (p105).

☼ Break for lunch at the restaurant of the **Musées Royaux d'Art et d'Histoire** (p106). Give yourself lots of time to experience the richness of the museum, where you can explore several epochs in world art and artefacts. Either laze away some time in the park, or detour, via the star-shaped **Berlaymont Building** (p111), to **Square Marie-Louise** (p109), surrounded by tall and gracious apartment blocks, some from the art nouveau period.

☾ This is not the greatest area for a night out, but **L'Atelier Européen** (p112) is a swish dinner stop. Otherwise, lively Place Jourdan offers great restaurants, bars, pizzas and a classic *frites* stand.

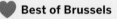 **Top Sights**

Parc du Cinquantenaire (p104)

Musées Royaux d'Art et d'Histoire (p106)

♥ **Best of Brussels**

Best for Haute Cuisine
Stirwen (p112)

L'Atelier Européen (p112)

Best Green Spaces
Parc du Cinquantenaire (p104)

Parc Léopold (p111)

Getting There

Ⓜ The **metro** is the best option to reach this area. The closest stop for the museums is Mérode, while to explore the EU sights head to Schuman. For Sq Marie-Louise get off at Maelbeek.

◉ Top Sights
Parc du Cinquantenaire

For all the functionality of the EU district, the area retains graceful parks and squares, most notably the Parc du Cinquantenaire: flanking it are some standout museums showcasing everything from sarcophagi to Harley Davidsons. The Cinquantenaire itself is a triumphal arch reminiscent of Paris' Arc de Triomphe. It was designed to celebrate Belgium's 50th anniversary (*cinquantenaire* in French) in 1880, but it took so long to build that by that date only a temporary plaster version was standing. The full arch wasn't completed till 1905.

Map p108, E3

Rue de la Loi & Rue Belliard

Ⓜ Mérode

Parc du Cinquantenaire

Don't Miss

Maison Cauchie

The famous **Maison Cauchie** (☎ 02-733 86 84; www.cauchie.be; Rue des Francs 5; adult/child €5/free; ⏰ 10am-1pm & 2-5.30pm 1st Sat & Sun of each month, plus 6pm-9pm most evenings May-Aug) is an art nouveau treasure, whose stunning 1905 facade is lavishly adorned with stylised female figures, the rose motif picked up in a spherical window with a tiny balcony. Book ahead to see the fabulous sgraffito-adorned rooms upstairs.

Musée Royal de l'Armée et d'Histoire Militaire

One for military buffs, the **Musée Royal de l'Armée et d'Histoire Militaire** (Royal Museum of the Armed Forces and of Military History; ☎ 02-737 78 11; www.klm-mra.be; Parc du Cinquantenaire 3; admission free, audio guide €3; ⏰ 9am-noon & 1-4.45pm Tue-Sun; Ⓜ Mérode) houses an extensive array of weaponry, uniforms, vehicles, warships, paintings and documentation dating from the Middle Ages through to Belgian independence and the mid-20th century.

Autoworld

Prior to WWII Belgium had a thriving auto industry, and the coolest of car collections on display at **Autoworld** (www.autoworld.be; adult/concession/BrusselsCard €9/6/free; ⏰ 10am-6pm Apr-Sep, 10am-5pm Oct-Mar; Ⓜ Mérode) is its legacy. Here you can see some 400 vehicles (Model T Fords, Citroen 2CVs and much more, through to the 1970s), housed in a stunning 1880 steel structure. Notice the Harley Davidson that the present king gifted to Belgium's police force when he decided his biker days were over.

☑ Top Tips

▶ The top of the Cinquantenaire Arcade provides sweeping city views. You access it via the military museum either by steps or a lift.

▶ In summer, the Arcade forms the curious backdrop to a drive-in cinema screen; check with the tourist board for program details.

▶ In the park itself, look out for the Pavillon Horta to the northwest. You won't find any of the architect's trademark motifs in this rather solid neoclassical structure though: it was his first public commission.

▶ Consider timing your visit for a Tuesday, so you can factor in an evening trip to the Maison Cauchie.

✗ Take a Break

There's a great collection of cafes, restaurants and bars on Place Jourdan, including the city's most famous *frites* stand, Maison Antoine (p112).

Top Sights
Musées Royaux d'Art et d'Histoire

Few Belgians realise there's a treasure trove lurking within this cavernous antiquities museum. The astonishingly rich global collection ranges from Ancient Egyptian sarcophagi and Meso-American masks to Russian icons and wooden bicycles. Visually attractive spaces include the medieval stone carvings set around a neo-Gothic cloister and the soaring Corinthian columns (convincing fibreglass props) that surround a mosaic from Roman Syria.

Map p108, D3

☎ 02-741 72 11

www.kmkg-mrah.be

Parc du Cinquantenaire 10

adult/concession/child €5/4/free

⏰ 9.30am-5pm Tue-Fri, 10am-5pm Sat & Sun

Ⓜ Mérode

Sculpture at the Musées Royaux d'Art et d'Histoire

Don't Miss

Antiquity

The rich variety of antiquities ranges from ancient Egyptian treasures, including 10 mummies and sarcophagi, to a large collection of Belgian artefacts from the first human settlements in the region. The highlight, though, is the Roman Syrian gallery, where a large and vivid 415-AD mosaic depicts tigers being speared and lions being hunted down by dogs.

European Decorative Arts

Many people will make a beeline for the glorious art nouveau and art deco objects, whose display cases were designed by Victor Horta. There are also Romanesque, Renaissance and baroque galleries, and a changing collection of tapestries. A whole gallery is devoted to clocks and astronomical devices and there's also a delightful assemblage of 35 painted sledges from the 1930s and '40s.

Non-European Civilisations

The scope of this section is impressive, taking in pre-Colombian art, American Indian headdresses, Jainist, Hindu and Buddhist deities, Chinese ceramics, rare Islamic textiles, Byzantine art and Coptic fabrics. Perhaps the most startling exhibit, though, is the woefully displaced Easter Island sculpture, a six-tonne stone giant collected on a Franco-Belgian expedition in the 1930s.

Tintin Trail

The museum is a must for those on the Tintin trail: a goulish skeleton mummy inspired *The Seven Crystal Balls*, while the Arumba fetish in *The Broken Ear* was based on a wooden votive figure displayed in the galleries.

☑ **Top Tips**

▶ Labelling in Musées Royaux is in French and Dutch so the English-language audio guide (€3 extra) is worth considering.

▶ Have a clear idea what you want to see before arriving or the sheer scope can prove overwhelming. Individual highlights are flagged on the website in the 'masterpieces online' section.

▶ Admission is free on the first Wednesday of the month, after 1pm.

▶ On Sunday you can enjoy brunch at the museum restaurant before tackling the galleries.

▶ The museum shop sells scholarly guides to the gallery collections, as well as the usual memorabilia and gifts.

✖ **Take a Break**

The museum has an acclaimed and up-market bistro, **Le Midi Cinquante** (☎02-735 87 54; mains €13-15; ⏱9.30am-4.30pm, closed Mon), whose terrace looks onto the park.

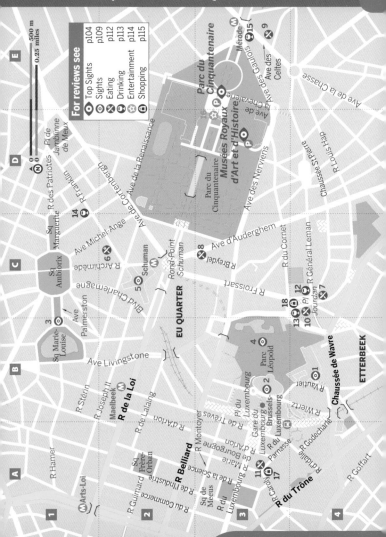

500 m
0.25 miles

For reviews see

◎ Top Sights p104
◎ Sights p109
✖ Eating p112
🅿 Drinking p113
🅿 Entertainment p114
🛍 Shopping p115

Parc du Cinquantenaire

Mérode Ⓜ

Ave des Gaulos

Ave des Celtes

Ave de la Chasse

Musées Royaux d'Art et d'Histoire

Parc du Cinquantenaire

Ave de Chevalerie

Ave des Nerviens

R Louis Hap

Chaussée St-Pierre

Ave de la Renaissance

Ave Cortenbergh

Ave Michel-Ange

R de l'Artiki

R des Patriotes

R Marguerite

Sq Marguerite

Pl de Jamblinne de Meux

R Archimède

Sq Ambiorix

Ave Palmerston

Sq Marie-Louise

Ave Livingstone

Blvd Charlemagne

Schuman Ⓜ

Rond-Point Schuman

Ave d'Auderghem

R Froissart

R du Cornet

R Général Leman

R du Cornet

R Jourdan

EU QUARTER

Parc Léopold

R Vautier

ETTERBEEK

Chaussée de Wavre

R Stévin

R Joseph II

Maelbeek Ⓜ

R de la Loi

R de Laling

R d'Arlon

R Belliard

R de la Science

R de Trèves

R Montoyer

R de Bourgogne

Pl du Luxembourg

Gare du Luxembourg

Brussels-Luxembourg

R du Luxembourg

R Marie de Bourgogne

R Parnasse

R Wiertz

R Godecharle

R d'Idalie

R du Trône

R Goffart

R Hamer

Arts-Loi Ⓜ

R Guimard

R du Commerce

R de l'Industrie

Sq Frère-Orban

Sq de Meeus

R du Luxembourg

R Caroly

R du Trône

Sights

Musée des Sciences Naturelles

MUSEUM

1 ⊙ Map p108, B4

Thought-provoking and highly interactive, this museum has far more than the usual selection of stuffed animals. The undoubted highlight is a unique 'family' of iguanodons – 10m-high dinosaurs found in a Hainaut coalmine back in 1878. A computer simulation shows the mudslide that might have covered them, sand-boxes allow you to play dino hunter and multilingual videos offer a wonderfully nuanced exploration of recent palaeontology. (☎02-627 42 38; www.naturalsciences. be; Rue Vautier 29; adult/concession/child/Brusselscard €7/6/4.50/free; ⊙9.30am-5pm Tue-Fri, 10am-6pm Sat & Sun; ☐38 (direction Homborch; departs from next to Gare Centrale) to De Meeus on Rue du Luxembourg)

EU Parliament

BUILDING

2 ⊙ Map p108, B3

Inside this decidedly dated blue-glass building (completed only just over a decade ago) political junkies can sit in on a parliamentary session in the huge debating chamber known as the hemicycle; tours of the building are available when parliament is not sitting. The tours (using multilingual headphones) start at the **visitor's centre** attached to the Paul-Henri Spaak section of the parliament.

(☎02-284 34 57; www.europarl.europa.eu; Rue Wiertz 43; admission free; ⊙tours 10am & 3pm Mon-Thu, 10am Fri; ☐38 (direction Homborch; departs from next to Gare Centrale) to De Meeus on Rue du Luxembourg)

Square Marie-Louise

SQUARE

3 ⊙ Map p108, B1

You can feed the ducks at this pretty tree-lined pond surrounded by greenery and circled by tall and handsome mansions. There's a fake grotto and,

---

✓ Top Tip

Art Nouveau in the EU

Private **Hôtel Van Eetvelde** (Map p108, C1; Ave Palmerston 2-4) can only be accessed on an ARAU tour (p144). While the outside of this building is not Brussels' most gripping, its interior is a Horta masterpiece studded with exotic timbers and sporting a central glass dome infused with African-inspired plant motifs. Its owner, Baron Van Eetvelde, was at that time Minister for the Congo and, not coincidentally, the country's highest-paid civil servant.

Narrow **Maison St-Cyr** (Map p108, C1; Sq Ambiorix 11) has a classic 1903 facade that's remarkable for its naturalistic copper-framed window, filigree balconies and a circular upper portal. It's crowned by a devil-may-care topknot of extravagantly twisted ironwork.

Understand

Belgian break up

It's perhaps an irony that Belgium, with its central role in the – ideally – consensual politics of the European Commission and NATO, is linguistically and culturally at odds with itself. Nowhere is this split more evident than in bilingual Brussels, where there is real division between the numerically dominant French speakers and the proud Flemish residents.

In 2006, Francophone public broadcaster RTBF interrupted programming with footage of a reporter outside the Royal Palace, claiming that Flanders had declared independence and King Albert had left the country. Only after half an hour did the program-makers admit the hoax, stating that they intended to demonstrate the importance of the ongoing political debate around the future of Belgium.

Division and Monarchy

The question of whether Belgium will hold together or split apart is never far away. Brussels, with its geographical location in Flanders, its linguistic orientation in Wallonia, and its status as the capital of the EU, is the major sticking point. There is also the question of what would happen to Belgium's tiny German-speaking region, as well as the fate of Belgium's monarchy, although surveys have shown that many younger Belgians believe a monarchy is unnecessary in the 21st century.

Brussels as a City State

If Belgium did split, it's unlikely that Wallonia would join France, or that Flanders would join the Netherlands. Instead, one model for the future is that Flanders and Wallonia would each become independent, with Brussels becoming its own city state, possibly administered by the EU. Certainly, the economic and legal unification provided by the EU makes it more viable than at any other time in modern history for such small nations to exist independently.

Belgian Quality

Still, the general sentiment in most quarters is that people don't want Belgium to split. Aside from personal attachment, a key pragmatic reason is that 'Belgian' has become a byword for quality (think 'Belgian chocolate' or 'Belgian beer'). Some feel this reputation would be diminished if Flanders and Wallonia split into separate countries, since these are lesser-known names internationally. For the foreseeable future at least, it seems likely that Belgium will endure.

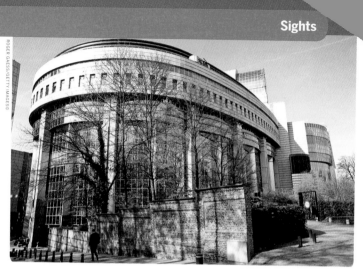

ROGER GAESS/GETTY IMAGES©

The European Parliament building

on the east side of the square, a couple of lovely art nouveau houses. (off Ave Palmerston-Laan; Ⓜ Maelbeek)

Parc Léopold

PARK

4 ⊙ Map p108, B3

Steep-sloping Parc Léopold was Brussels Zoo till 1880 and now forms an unexpectedly pleasant oasis hidden away just behind the EU Parliament. Fine century-old buildings like the attractive Solvay Library and Jacqmain School are closed to the public and the Musée Antoine Wiertz, displaying Wiertz's frenzied 19th-century hell scenes, isn't for everyone. But the Musée des Sciences Naturelles alone justifies the trip. (Ⓜ Schuman)

Berlaymont Building

BUILDING

5 ⊙ Map p108, C2

Although the 1967-built, star-shaped Berlaymont building that houses the European Commission isn't open to the public, information panels outside give a succinct overview of the structure of the EU, its role in the European capital, and the reasons for Brussels' predominant status. Inside the gargantuan building are the EU commissioners and their teams, numbering 2700 officials in all. (Rue de la Loi 200; Ⓜ Schuman)

Eating

L'Atelier Européen

BELGIAN $$

6 | Map p108, C2

Tucked down an alley and fronted by a hedged courtyard, this former wine warehouse has a pared-down but sophisticated menu of meat and fish dishes, such as sautéed veal and grilled sea bass, with a couple (but only a couple) of offerings for vegetarians. Wine is given its due, with a well-chosen list and monthly specials. (☑02-734 91 40; Rue Franklin 28; ⏲noon-2.30pm & 6.30-10pm Mon-Fri; Ⓜ Schuman)

Stirwen

FRENCH $$$

7 | Map p108, C4

A long-established Franco-Belgian restaurant that's popular with a discerning EU crowd. The decor is rather dark and conservative, but the classic and traditional French cooking is always reliable. (☑02-640 85 41; www. stirwen.be; Chaussée Saint-Pierre 15; ⏲noon-midnight Mon-Fri; Ⓜ Schuman)

Au Bain Marie

ITALIAN $$

8 | Map p108, C3

Dine amongst the Eurocrats near EU HQ. Despite its French name, Au Bain Marie is actually a casual and welcoming Italian restaurant. In summer, the best place to sit is outside on the terrace. (☑02-280 48 88; Rue Breydel 46; ⏲noon-10pm Mon-Fri)

Local Life

Maison Antoine

Brussels can be divided into two kinds of people: not French- and Dutch-speaking, nor locals and expats, but rather those who swear by this chip shop versus those who pledge allegiance to the caravan on Place Flagey. **Maison Antoine's** (Map p108, C4; Place Jourdan; small chips from €2; ⏲11.30am-1am Sun-Thu, 11.30am-2am Fri & Sat; Ⓜ Schuman) chips are twice-fried in beef fat, so they're twice as delicious; you'll see dignitaries, tourists and the odd celeb queuing for a coneful. If you'd prefer to eat your *frites* accompanied by a beer, you can bring them along to many of the bars on the Place Jourdan.

Capoue

ICE CREAM $

9 | Map p108, E3

Capoue has great ice cream in a dizzying variety of flavours, including *speculoos*, Belgium's trademark biscuit. They also serve frozen yoghurt and snacks. (☑02-705 37 10; www.capoue. com; Avenue des Celtes 36; ⏲noon-10pm)

L'Esprit de Sel

BRASSERIE $$

10 | Map p108, C4

Located on the nicest square in the area, this Belgian/French place features swish decor and provides a good variety of local beers as well as hearty brasserie fare such as *moules* and beef carpaccio. (☑02-230 60 40; www.espritde sel.be; Place Jourdan 52; ⏲noon-midnight)

Poivre et Sel
ITALIAN $$

11 🍴 Map p108, A3

This popular Italian place is situated in the heart of the EU area – be sure to book in advance. Good service and fresh ingredients: try the lobster ravioli! (📞02-503 46 93; www.poivre-et-sel. be; Rue du Parnasse 2 ; ⏰noon-2.30pm & 6-10.30pm Mon-Fri)

Drinking

Café de l'Autobus
BAR

12 🍺 Map p108, C4

Old-timers' bar opposite Maison Antoine, the city's most famous *friture*. The owners don't mind if you demolish a cone of *frites* while downing a beer or two. On Sunday it's a breather for vendors from the Place Jourdan food market. (📞02-230 63 16; Place Jourdan; Ⓜ Schuman)

Chez Bernard
BAR

13 🍺 Map p108, C4

This is very much an old-fashioned and classic Belgian bar, where beer is the main attraction. Ask for their advice if you're stuck choosing a brew. (📞02-231 10 73; Place Jourdan 47; ⏰11am-midnight; Ⓜ Schuman)

Piola Libri
BAR

14 🍺 Map p108, D1

Italian Eurocrats relax after work on sofas, pavement tables or in the tiny triangle of back garden and enjoy free

---

Understand
'French' Fries

Just as the Brussels waffle actually originates from Ghent, **French fries** in fact hail from Belgium. The misnomer evolved during WWI in West Flanders, when English officers heard their Belgian counterparts speaking French while consuming fries and mistook their nationality (military orders were given in French, even to Dutch-only-speaking soldiers, with tragic consequences).

Fries here are made from Belgian- or Netherlands-grown *bintje* potatoes. They're hand-cut about 1cm thick – any smaller and they absorb too much oil and burn – they're cooked first at a lower temperature then again at a higher temperature to become crispy on the outside while remaining soft inside. This double-cooking is what distinguish the Belgian chip from its flabbier counterparts elsewhere. Typically, *frites* are served in a paper cone and liberally smothered in a rich sauce. There are dozens of sauces including the classic, mayonnaise. If you're bewildered by the choice, take a chance with Andalouse, which is like very mildly spiced thousand-island dressing.

ROGER GAESS/GETTY IMAGES©

Parc Léopold (p111)

tapas-style snacks with chilled white wines at this convivial bookshop/cafe/bar. It has an eclectic program of readings and DJ nights. (☎02-736 93 91; www.piolalibri.be; Rue Franklin 66; ⏰noon-8pm Mon-Fri, noon-6pm Sat, closed Aug; 🛜; Ⓜ Schuman)

La Terrasse
BRASSERIE

15 🍽 Map p108, E3

Handy for the Cinquantenaire, this wood-panelled classic cafe has a tree-shaded terrace and makes an ideal refreshment stop after a hard day's museuming; for something different, try the 'beer of the month'. Snacks, pancakes, ice creams, breakfasts and decent pub meals are all available at various times. (☎02-732 28 51; www.brasserielaterrasse.be; Ave des Celtes 1; beers €2.40-4.50; ⏰8am-midnight Mon-Sat, 10am-midnight Sun; Ⓜ Mérode)

Entertainment

Arcade du Cinquantenaire
CINEMA

16 ⭐ Map p108, D3

Ask at the tourist office for the program of summertime drive-in movie screenings (with headphones available for nondrivers) under the Arcade du Cinquantenaire triumphal arch in the Parc du Cinquantenaire. (⏰summer only; Ⓜ Mérode)

Shopping

Crush Wine
WINE

17 🔒 Map p108, A3

Brussels is too self-respecting to have a Fosters-spouting Aussie-themed bar, but international enough to have this wondrous cellar stocking over 190 Australian wines (the most comprehensive selection in Europe). Look out for rare drops from Tasmania and dozens of Margaret River reds. There are daily tastings, tapas and regular events; call ahead for the schedule of Saturday openings. (📞02 502 66 97; www.crushwine.be; Rue Caroly 39; ◷11am-7pm Mon-Fri plus 1 Sat per month; Ⓜ Trône)

Place Jourdan Market
MARKET

18 🔒 Map p108, C4

Place Jourdan hosts a small Sunday-morning market selling food and clothes. It's a great spot to do some browsing and then relax with a coffee on the square. (Place Jourdan; ◷7am-2pm Sun; Ⓜ Schuman)

Top Sights
Musée Horta

Getting There

🚌 92 runs from Place Louise (15 min; every 15 min)

Ⓜ Horta

🚌 See the Musée Horta and other art nouveau houses on the ARAU bus tour

The exterior doesn't give much away, but Victor Horta's former home (designed and built 1898–1901) is an art nouveau jewel. Bathed in warm colours, the ground-floor living areas incorporate gleaming floor-to-ceiling tiling, while upstairs you can see Horta's personalised touches in the small, intimate rooms. The lower level offers an overview of his work, including a model of his magnificent Maison du Peuple which tragically met with the wrecking ball.

Interior at the Musée Horta

Don't Miss

Stairwell

The stairwell is the structural triumph of the house – follow the playful knots and curlicues of the banister, which become more exuberant as you ascend, ending at a tangle of swirls and glass lamps at the skylight, glazed with citrus-coloured and plain glass. Metal arches and girders unify the design from the top to the bottom of the house, and rooms open out to the front and back, giving a great sense of space and light.

Dining Room

Floor mosaics, glittering stained glass, and ceramic brick walls reflect the light in this superbly harmonious room, rich with swirling American ash furniture, glowing brass and a pink-and-orange colour scheme. The room opens into a salon, with glass doors creating a sense of flow into the garden beyond.

Bedrooms

There is more honey-coloured American ash in Horta's bedroom, where a closet reveals a discreet and handy urinal. Adjoining is a reconstructed bathroom with a very grand water heater and shower. Horta's daughter's room has a pretty winter garden, while you can only envy people who were invited to stay in the guest bedroom at the top of the house: the swirly brass door-handle is a pleasure in itself.

Exterior

As is typical of Horta's work, the exterior is relatively austere, though nice to contemplate once you've been inside – look out for the dragonfly-shaped railing of the guestroom window and the aesthetic/industrial metal balcony.

☎ 02-543 04 90

www.hortamuseum.be

Rue Américaine 25

adult/child €7/3.50

⊙ 2-5.30pm Tue-Sun

☑ Top Tips

▶ For detailed coverage, buy the excellent museum guide (€10).

▶ Visits are limited to 45 people – arrive early to avoid queuing.

▶ Guided tours in English are available on request.

▶ Another option for seeing the house – and other art nouveau buildings – with an expert guide, is to book one of the bus tours operated by Arau (02-219 33 45; www.arau.org; 3hr; €17).

✗ Take a Break

Try friendly bistro **SiSiSi** (☎ 02-538 58 18; Chaussée de Charleroi 174; ⊙ 10am-midnight), or have a glass of wine and a cheese platter at stylish **Oeno tk** (☎ 02-534 64 34; ⊙ 11am-8pm Mon & Tue, till 10.30pm Wed-Sat).

Local Life
A Stroll in the Marolles

Getting There

The glass elevator from Place Poelaert, in front of the Palais de Justice, whisks you down the steep hill to the Marolles.

Ⓜ Gare du Midi and Porte de Hal are the best **metro** stations.

Brussels' partially gentrified working-class area, the Marolles, is known for its colourful dialect and down-to-earth watering holes. To appreciate the area's roots head to Place du Jeu-de-Balle, or pop into a neighbourhood bar. Crumbling brick chimneys are another remnant of the area's industrial past. Visit on Sunday for the Gare du Midi market (though the brewery will be closed): to take in morning Mass at the church visit these sights in a different order!

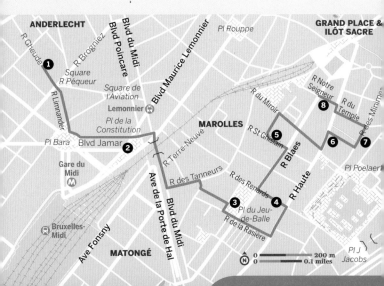

❶ Taste Some Brews

If you're in the area from Monday to Saturday, start your tour at **Musée Bruxellois de la Gueuze** (📞02-521 49 28; www.cantillon.be; Rue Gheude 56; admission €5; 🕙8.30am-5pm Mon-Fri, 10am-5pm Sat; Ⓜ Gare du Midi), which takes you behind the scenes of the production of these unique lambic beers. And of course, you get to taste some, too.

❷ Wander Gare du Midi Market

If you're visiting on a Sunday, head to the Gare du Midi **market** (🕙6am-1pm Sun; Ⓜ Gare du Midi), said to be the biggest in Europe. This sprawl of colourful stalls has an international flavour, with exotic North African and Mediterranean spices, cheeses, meats, clothing and leather goods.

❸ Shop at Jeu-de-Balle Flea Market

The quintessential Marolles experience is haggling at this chaotic **flea market** (Place du Jeu-de-Balle; 🕙7am-2pm; Ⓜ Porte de Hal or 🚊 Lemonnier). Weekends see it at its liveliest, but for the best bargains head here early morning midweek. Stop for a coffee at **Le Marsellais** (📞02-503 00 83; Rue Blaes 163; 🕙8am-midnight Tue-Sun) on the north-east corner of the square: 55 varieties of pastis are served here.

❹ Walk up Rue des Renard

This narrow street exemplifies how the area is changing – on the left heading uphill are trendy vintage and retro shops, on the right cottages and tra-ditional restaurants. At the top you'll often find a vestige of the old Marolles: a cart selling little pots of snails.

❺ View Horta's Jardin d'Enfants

This lovely Horta **building** (Rue St-Ghislain 40) was designed as a school, and is still used as such, so you'll only be able to view it from the outside. Look for sinuous plant motifs, a playful tower, and stripes of grey and pale stone.

❻ Check out the Brueghel House

There is a **museum** (📞02-513 89 40; Rue Haute 132) in this step-gabled house where Pieter Brueghel the Elder lived and died, but it's only open by reservation; phone ahead or check with the tourist office for details.

❼ See St-Jeanne-et-Étienne aux Minimes

The area's **church** (📞02-511 93 84; Rue des Minimes 62; 🚊27) is a huge, sooty and weather-beaten baroque structure, completed in 1715. If you visit on Sunday at 11.30am you can go to Mass – the acoustics of the ribbed cupola are very good, and Mass features either Gregorian chants or Bach cantatas.

❽ Dine at L'Idiot du Village

Booking ahead is essential to secure a table at the colourful **L'Idiot du Village** (📞02-502 55 82; Rue Notre Seigneur 19; 🕙noon-2pm & 7.30-11pm Mon-Fri; Ⓜ Louise), secluded on a little side street near the Place du Jeu-de-Balle. The Belgian dishes are rich and aromatic (lots of herbs) and portions are generous.

Local Life
Shopping in Ste-Catherine

Ste-Catherine is a byword for what's hippest and happening right now in the capital. The main drag, Rue Antoine Dansaert, forms the focal point for Brussels' rapidly rising fashion scene, featuring avant-garde home-grown designers, while Rue de Flandre and Rue Léon Lepage host smaller and quirkier boutiques.

Getting There

M The nearest **metro** station is Bourse, but it'll take you no more than 15 minutes to **walk** here from the Grand Place.

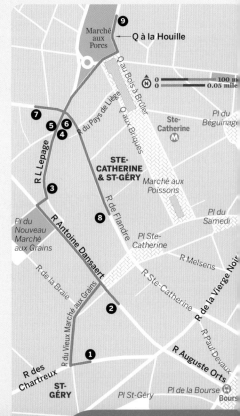

Marché aux Porcs

Q à la Houille ⑨

Q au Bois à Brûler

0 ___ 100 m
0 ___ 0.05 mile

Pl du Béguinage

Ste-Catherine **M**

⑦

⑤ ⑥
④

R du Pays de Liège

Q aux Briques

STE-CATHERINE & ST-GÉRY

R L Lepage

③

Marché aux Poissons

R de Flandre

⑧

Pl du Samedi

Pl du Nouveau Marché aux Grains

R Antoine Dansaert

Pl Ste-Catherine

R Melsens

R Ste-Catherine

R de la Braie

R du Vieux Marché aux Grains

②

R de la Vierge Noire

R Paul Devaux

R Auguste Orts

①

R des Chartreux

ST-GÉRY

Pl St-Géry

Pl de la Bourse

Bours

❶ Vintage Treasures at Gabriele

For amazing vintage finds try eccentric, elegant **Gabriele** (☎02-512 67 43; gabrielevintage.com; Rue des Chartreux 27; ⏰1-6.30pm Mon & Tue, 11am-6.30pm Wed-Sat). There's a gorgeous jumble of cocktail dresses, hats, Chinese shawls and accessories; only original clothes from the '20s to '80s are stocked.

❷ Book Shopping at Passa Porta

This stylish **bookshop** (☎02-226 04 54; www.passaporta.be; Rue Antoine Dansaert 46; ⏰11am-7pm Tue-Sat, noon-6pm Sun) located down an alley has a small but classy English-language section. Look out for the leaflet listing literary events, many of which are hosted in English.

❸ Designer Garb and Vinyl at Mapp

One of the coolest stores in this area, **Mapp** (☎02-551 17 67; thisismapp.com; Rue Léon Lepage 5; ⏰11am-7pm Mon-Sat, 2pm-6pm Sun) has a fast-changing stock of clothes, accessories, books, CDs and vinyl. They specialise in young and up-and-coming designers. Too cool for school, though the staff are friendly.

❹ Romantic Fashion at Just In Case

Poetic and feminine garments inspired by the past, with vintage-style shapes. The beautiful clothes at **Just In Case** (justincase.b; Rue Léon Lepage 63; ⏰11am-7pm Tue-Sat) are arranged by colour: electric blue, coral and orange.

❺ Bargains at Outlet Privejoke

Casual fashion for men and women usually has a hefty price tag, though not at this small **outlet store** (Rue Léon Lepage 30; ⏰2pm-7pm Wed-Sun). Good for functional jackets and separates.

❻ Stop for a Drink at Au Laboureur

Sample old Brussels when you need some refreshment: this characterful corner **bar** (Rue de Flandre 108; beer €1.60; ⏰9.30am-10pm) is a great beer-stop.

❼ Quirky Fashion at Lowi

Idiosyncratic fashion and accessories are the order of the day at **Lowi** (www.lowi.be; Rue de Flandre 124; ⏰11am-7pm Tue-Sat), including covetable ceramic and porcelain jewellery.

❽ Cooking Heaven at Pimpinelle

This cute **boutique** (www.pimpinelle.be; Rue de Flandre 57; ⏰ noon-6.30pm Mon-Sat) sells pale ceramics and utilitarian tin plates, plus cake tins, pots and pans and scales. They also run cookery workshops in the attractively tiled back room.

❾ Arts and Crafts at Micro Marché

Round off your shopping with something different: the alternative and affordable handmade crafts at boho **Micro Marché** (Quai à la Houille 9; ⏰4pm-9pm Fri, 11am-7pm Sat & Sun). The industrial courtyard has been converted into a performance and exhibition space, plus there's a travellers' cafe, all of which makes it a bit of a hub in the area.

The Best of
Bruges & Brussels

Bruges and Brussels' Best Walks

Bruges and Brussels' Best...

Varieties of Belgian Beer
MARTIN MOOS/GETTY IMAGES©

Best Walks
Art Nouveau Brussels

The Walk

Art nouveau is the signature architectural style of Brussels, and its most significant exponent was Victor Horta (1861–1947), an architectural chameleon mostly remembered for daring, light-suffused buildings using trademark elements of wrought iron and glass. His celebrated Maison du Peuple was torn down in 1965, but surviving masterpieces can be explored on this route, along with some lovely buildings by his contemporaries. Only Musée Horta is open to the public – to see some interiors take one of ARAU's excellent **tours** (p144).

Start Porte de Hal; Ⓜ Porte de Hal

Finish Avenue Louise

Length 3km; two hours

Take a Break

End your walk by strolling to Place Flagey, where you can have a leisurely drink at super-hip **Café Belga** (☎02-640 3508; Place Flagey 18; ⏰8am-2am).

Interior at the Musée Horta

RICHARD BRYANT/ARCAID/CORBIS©

❶ La Porteuse d'Eau

Head down Chaussée de Waterloo from the fairy-tale **Porte de Hal**, and turn right onto Avenue Jean Volders. At no 48 you can have a coffee at this classic art nouveau *café* featuring spectacular stained glass and ornate wooden booths.

❷ Hôtel Winssinger

Rue de la Victoire soon takes you past the **Hôtel Winssinger**, a sober Horta building that, typically, does not call attention to itself. Look for the characteristic pale stone, as well as the use of metal around the windows and the dainty swirling balconies.

❸ Musée Victor Horta

You may want to visit **Horta's house** (p116) separately to give yourself plenty of time. But do pause to admire the characteristically simple exterior, featuring a playful dragonfly motif. The interior is flooded with light from above and alive with swirling lines.

❹ Les Hiboux & Hôtel Hannon

Following avenue Brugmann brings you to two delightful adjoining art nouveau buildings: Édouard Pelseneer's red-brick **Les Hiboux**, surmounted by two Gothic owls, and Jules Brunfaut's **Hôtel Hannon**, graced by stone friezes and stained glass.

❺ Maison & Atelier Dubois

Across the road at no 80 is another Horta building, commissioned by the designer Fernand Dubois. It's now the Cuban embassy, but you can see from the outside how the large windows flood the studio with light.

❻ Hankar buildings

Head up Rue Africaine to admire Paul Hankar's buildings on Rue Defacqz, externally more exuberant constructs than Horta's. The examples at nos 48, 50 and 71 are adorned with friezes and gleaming frescos.

❼ Hôtel Tassel

Nearby Rue Paul-Émile Janson is the site of Horta's first truly art nouveau house, the 1893 **Hôtel Tassel**. Horta designed the mosaics, stained glass, woodwork – even the door handles.

❽ Hôtel Solvay

Turn right onto Avenue Louise and head down to **Hôtel Solvay**. Again, Horta designed every element of the house, incorporating luxurious materials such as tropical wood, bronze and onyx, though the exterior gives away little of the rich decorative scheme inside.

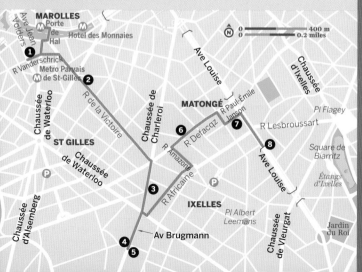

Best Walks
Bruges' Parks and Canals

🏃 The Walk

This circular walk takes you from the heart of Bruges to some of its most charming green spaces: the Koningin Astridpark with its little bandstand, the elongated park along Gentpoortvest, spacious Minnewater and the attractive courtyard of the Begijnhof. Beyond this point you circle back to the more touristy environs of the Vismarkt. An excellent patisserie en route provides perfect picnic fodder.

Start Vismarkt

Finish Vismarkt

Length 3km; two hours

✖ Take a Break

This route features the splendid little **Patisserie Schaeverbeke** (☎050 33 31 82; Schaarstraat 2), piled with creamy fruity cakes, croissants and fresh fragrant bread. Stock up here for a picnic near the Minnewater; you can also buy fresh fruit at the greengrocer across the road.

Rotunda at the Koningin Astridpark

❶ Vismarkt

The handsome colonnaded 1821 **fish market** (p41) is still open for business most days. Several seafood restaurants here back onto pretty Huidenvettersplein, where archetypal Bruges buildings including the old tanners' guildhouse are located. To start the walk, exit the south end of the market.

❷ Koningin Astridpark

From the Vismarkt, head south down J Suvéestraat to the little-visited but attractive **Koningin Astridpark**, named for the Swedish wife of King Léopold of Belgium – you can see her bust in the corner of the park, as well as a bandstand. Exit the park by the Gothic-revival Magdalen Church and detour to the scrumptious patisserie at Schaarstraat 2 before heading down Willemijnendreef.

❸ Gentpoort

Turn right at the end of the street to reach **Gentpoort**, one of the town's four medieval

LATITUDESTOCK/GETTY IMAGES©

gateways. From here, a pleasant footpath leads through the greenery along the water's edge.

④ Minnewater Park

You emerge at the **Minnewater Park** (p57), a scenic green space with orderly flower beds and secluded paths. It's hard to believe that the serene lake here, now known to Bruges-dwellers as the 'Lake of Love', was once the inner harbour of the city where exotic cargoes of wool, wine, spices and silks were unloaded.

⑤ Wijngaardplein

Head up to **Wijngaardplein**, a touristy but still irresistible square ringed by *cafés* and featuring a horse-head fountain where the city's carriage horses are watered. The *cafés* here are a little on the pricey side, but the views are refreshing.

⑥ Begijnhof

Over the little arched bridge from the square, the 13th-century **Begijnhof** (p50) is one of the delights of Bruges, its whitewashed

buildings encircling a garden with tall trees and swaths of daffodils in spring. It's well worth visiting the house museum here, as well as the church. From the Begijnhof, cross the water and head

up Wijngaardstraat to turn left onto Katelijnestraat. Bear right onto Gruuthusestraat (which becomes Dijver) and head back to the Vismarkt.

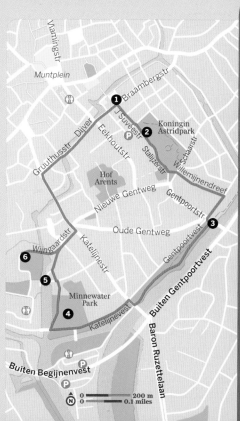

Best Walks
Back Streets of Western Bruges

🏃 The Walk

One of the chief pleasures of Bruges is to get off the beaten track and simply wander with no agenda. This short walk takes you from the Markt to the west of the city in a little loop, taking in some historic churches, Renaissance mansions and almshouses. There are no show-stopping sights, but you'll find fewer tourists and more tranquillity as soon as you head even a short distance away from the centre.

Start Markt

Finish Markt

Length 2.5km; 1.5 to two hours

🍴 Take a Break

Tucked just off Zuidzandstraat is the candlelit **Gran Kaffee De Passage** (Map p32, A8; 📞 050 34 02 32; www.passagebruges.com; Dweersstraat 26-28; mains €5-10; ⏱ 6-11pm), a nice place to stop before wending your way home; it serves hearty and filling Belgian food at bargain prices.

Eiermarkt

JON HICKS/CORBIS ©

❶ Markt

The walk starts at the **Markt** (p24), the heart of Bruges, with its fantastical neo-Gothic buildings and the tall Belfort tower looming above. From the square, take the street that leads to the southwest: Steenstraat, with its fine 17th-century facades.

❷ Simon Stevinplein

Here you can detour into the attractive square on the right-hand side, named for 16th-century Bruges mathematician and physician Simon Stevin, to sample the wares at the **Chocolate Line** (p62), run by Dominique Persoone, the city's most outrageous and innovative chocolatier.

❸ Zuidzandstraat

Resume your walk down Zuidzandstraat to 't Zand. Cross the square to bear left onto Boeveriestraat. Or you can detour here to another square, Beursplein, where live chickens, rabbits, food and flowers are sold at the market on Saturday mornings.

4 Boeverievest

Here the route joins the water, where you'll see the scenic old **Waterhuis**. Horses operated a wheel here to pull water out of the canal, which was then used to supply wells and breweries. Turn right to take the path through the stretch of parkland. Soon you come to the **Smedenpoort**, a 14th-century city gate.

5 Smedenstraat

Turn right back in the direction of the city centre up Smeden-

straat. Detour here up Kreupelenstraat or Kammakersstraat to see some typical Bruges almshouses.

6 Speelmansrei

Speelmansrei curves to the left, following the left bank of the canal for a stretch. Cross the canal and turn left onto Moerstraat, then right onto Ontvangersstraat. Head down and turn left onto bustling Noordzanstraat.

7 Eiermarkt

A final detour is to peek at little Muntplein off to the left, where locals gather to eat ice cream from **Da Vinci** (p37). Then you join the attractive *café*-encircled mini square of Eiermarkt, before returning to the spacious Markt.

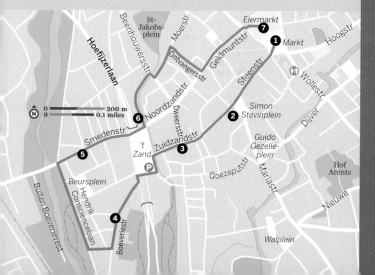

Best
Eating

Be sure to bring a healthy appetite with you – restaurants in Brussels and Bruges dish up a seemingly endless procession of delicious fare. What's more, Belgium boasts more Michelin stars per capita than anywhere in Europe. Many *cafés* (including bars and pubs) also serve hearty meals.

What to Eat

Breakfast in Flanders is a hearty affair of cured meats, cheeses, cereals and so on. At lunchtime many restaurants offer a *dagschotel*/*plat du jour* (dish of the day). Also watch for a 'menu of the day' (*dagmenu* in Dutch, or *menu du jour* in French). These set menus comprise three or more courses and work out cheaper than ordering individual courses à la carte. Some kitchens open as early as 6pm for dinner, but most don't get busy until at least a couple of hours later.

Mussels and Fries

If Belgium has a national dish, it is mussels (*mosselen* in Dutch, *moules* in French). Forget about using a fork to scoop out these much-loved molluscs; use an empty shell as a pincher to prise them out. Fries (*frieten* in Dutch, *frites* in French) are even more ubiquitous. Not only do they accompany mussels (and virtually any other dish), but they are easily Belgium's favourite snack.

Meat Lovers

Those of a delicate disposition, beware: Belgians' idea of *saignant* (rare) is meat dripping with blood; *à point* (medium) is what other nationalities consider rare, and *bien cuit* is the closest you'll get to well done. (These French terms are also used by Dutch speakers.)

JEAN-PIERRE DEGAS/HEMIS/CORBIS©

☑ Top Tips

Belgian specialities:
▶ *Bloedworst* (black pudding made with pig's blood, served with apple sauce)

▶ *Breugel Kop* (chunks of beef and tongue set in gelatine)

▶ *Filet américain* (raw minced beef)

▶ *Konijn met pruimen* (tender rabbit in sauce with prunes)

▶ *Paardefilet*/ *steak de cheval* (horse steak)

▶ *Paling in 't groen*/ *anguilles au vert* (eel in green herb sauce)

▶ *Stoemp* (mashed potato usually topped with a sausage)

Best for Belgian Food, Brussels

Brasserie de la Roue d'Or Sample suckling pig and steak. (p78)

Maison Antoine Allegedly the finest chips in town. (p112)

Dandoy The best place to sample Brussels biscuits. (p78)

Mokafé Authentic icing-sugar-sprinkled waffles. (p78)

Best for Belgian Food, Bruges

Den Dijver Excellent food cooked in Belgian beer. (p58)

In 't Nieuwe Museum Back street joint serving eel, steaks and casseroles. (p37)

Christophe Flemish fare, including many varieties of steak. (p60)

Restobières Belgian-beer-themed food. (p98)

Best for Haute Cuisine, Brussels

Café-Restaurant de l'Ogenblik Delightful old-town bistro. (p76)

La Maison du Cygne Fine dining on the Grand Place. (p79)

Stirwen Posh eating in the EU district. (p112)

Sea Grill The town's best seafood in a fancy hotel restaurant. (p79)

L'Atelier Européen Secluded and smart restaurant for the Euro set. (p112)

Best for Haute Cuisine, Bruges

De Karmeliet Complex and elegant food in a Michelin-starred restaurant. (p36)

Den Gouden Harynck Swish and sophisticated, in a gorgeous old building. (p59)

Best Ethnic Restaurants, Brussels

Kokob Ethopian food served in a welcoming atmosphere. (p78)

Easy Tempo Have a break from waffles and order a pizza. (p98)

Best for Seafood, Bruges

Den Gouden Karpel By the fish market, serving crab, shrimps and oysters. (p35)

De Stove Fish dishes, with everything caught daily. (p35)

Chagall Eel and *moules* are on the menu in this cosy place. (p36)

Best for Escaping the Crowds, Bruges

De Belegde Boterham Smart lunch spot patronised by locals. (p29)

L'Estaminet Friendly bistro just off the beaten track by the Koningin Astridpark. (p29)

De Windmolen Cute *café*/bar in the shadow of the St-Anna windmills. (p31)

De Stoepa Backstreet bistro with a tranquil terrace garden. (p58)

Best Drinking & Nightlife

You'll encounter a bewildering choice of Belgian beers and *jenevers* at just about every drinking establishment, but the best places to try these are specialist *'jenever cafés'* and 'beer pubs'. In bars and clubs, jazz is the style of live music you'll encounter most often. Look out for flyers in music shops, streetwear boutiques, bars and *cafés* about DJ nights, club fixtures and one-off parties.

ILPO MUSTO/ALAMY ©

Drinking Culture

At specialised drinking establishments, you'll be handed a thick menu detailing hundreds of varieties of beer. Wading through the menus is a Herculean feat: ask the staff for the flavours and characteristics you have in mind and be guided by them. Drinking establishments usually open around 10am; closing hours aren't restricted by law but simply depend on how busy it is on the night.

Where to Drink

Cafés always serve alcohol and some, though not all, also serve food. Places that do are sometimes classified as an *eetcafé* ('eating cafe') or a *grand café* (a larger, more elegant version of an *eetcafé*), and it's fine to just stop in for a drink even if you're not dining. You can also just pop in for a drink at a brasserie or bistro, although these are chiefly eateries. Anywhere that labels itself a bar generally only serves drinks. Likewise, a *herberg* (Dutch for 'tavern') is primarily a drinking spot. One of the most atmospheric *cafés* for drinking is the traditional *bruin café* ('brown cafe', sometimes called a *bruine kroeg*). So named for their wood panelling, interspersed with oversize mirrors, these small, cosy, old-fashioned pubs are prime places for mixing with locals.

☑ Top Tips

▶ Drinking with locals, you'll notice that everyone buys rounds (all but 'Bob' – the name Belgians give to a designated driver, thanks to a hugely successful campaign against drink-driving).

▶ You'll also notice locals ordering beers using a bizarre sign language.

▶ Remember to say 'Cheers!' – in Dutch, *schol* (or *gezondheid* – to your health), and in French, *santé*!

JEAN-BERNARD CARILLET/GETTY IMAGES©

Fruit-flavoured beer varieties

Best Specialist Beer Pubs, Brussels

À la Mort Subite Try the speciality *gueuze*. (p79)

Moeder Lambic Fontainas Hip bar serving artisanal beers. (p81)

La Fleur en Papier Doré Old-style pub, once frequented by Magritte. (p99)

Best Specialist Beer Pubs, Bruges

't Brugs Beertje Cosy and full of character, with a huge range of brews. (p61)

De Garre Brace your tastebuds for 11% Garre beer. (p39)

't Poatersgat Cellar bar with umpteen Trappist beers on offer. (p38)

Café Vlissinghe Simply unmissable: the oldest bar in the city. (p38)

Cambrinus Historic beer bar in a 17th-century gabled building. (p39)

Best Live Music Bars, Brussels

Le Cercle des Voyageurs Live jazz plus good food and wine. (p76)

Le Fonograf Cute daytime *café* and night-time music bar. (p80)

Music Village Long-established classy jazz bar. (p81)

Art Base Small venue for serious music lovers. (p82)

Best Live Music Bars, Bruges

Du Phare Blues and jazz venue at the north end of town. (p41)

Retsin's Lucifernum Live Latin music in extraordinary environs. (p40)

Est Wijnbar Sunday-night jazz in a cute little wine bar. (p38)

Best
Entertainment

Considering that it was an opera performance that sparked the revolution for Belgian independence, it's not surprising that the performing arts are celebrated across the country. Brussels boasts dozens of superb venues, but these are by no means limited to the capital: Bruges has its own state-of-the-art venue, the Concertgebouw. There are also some charming traditional puppet theatres, notably the Théâtre Royal de Toone.

HEMIS/ALAMY©

Belgian Cinema

The Belgian love of cinema seems easily explained by two things: the fact that nightlife doesn't start until late, and the climate. The country brims with cinemas, though the industry itself is underfunded compared to other art forms.

Homegrown Movies

An average of just two mainstream Belgian films are released per year, in addition to smaller, lower-budget independent releases. But Belgian directors are internationally renowned, chief among them brothers Luc and Jean-Pierre Dardenne: their film, *The Kid With a Bike*, won the Grand Prix at Cannes Film Festival in 2011, while harrowing *Rosetta* (1999) and the rather more uplifting *L'Enfant* (2005) were both awarded the Palme d'Or. Bruges itself also starred memorably on the silver screen in 2008's hilarious action-comedy, *In Bruges*.

Local Stars

Unlike its directors, Belgium's film stars generally aren't well known outside their own country, the exception being Brussels' action hero Jean-Claude Van Damme. Local stars include Vincent Grass, Natacha Amal and Matthias Schoenaerts.

Best for Theatre, Music and Dance, Brussels

BOZAR Magnificent Horta-designed concert hall. (p100)

Théâtre du Vaudeville Theatre, concerts and cabaret. (p83)

Théâtre Royal de la Monnaie Hear a concert where Belgium's revolution began. (p83)

AB Best for pop and rock acts. (p82)

Théâtre National Gleaming French-language theatre. (p83)

Cirque Royal Big-name bands, concerts and dance. (p100)

Recyclart Alternative and grafitti-covered arts venue (pictured above). (p101)

TRAVEL DIVISION IMAGES/ALAMY©

Concertgebouw, Bruges

Best for Theatre, Music and Dance, Bruges

Koninklijke Stadsschouwburg A grand venue for classical music, dance and theatre. (p40)

Concertgebouw This modern concert hall shows top-drawer music and dance. (p61)

Cactus Muziekcentrum World and modern music, plus its own music festival. (p62)

Best Cinemas, Brussels

Actor's Studio Hunt the alleys for this arthouse gem. (p82)

Cinéma Galeries Tucked away in the Galeries St-Hubert. (p82)

Cinematek Arthouse classics and silent films with live accompaniment. (p100)

Best Belgian Film Festivals

Anima, Brussels & Ghent (http://folioscope. awn.com) In February, Brussels' animated film festival attracts top-quality shorts and features.

Cinema Novo Film Festival, Bruges (www. cinemanovo.be) In March, independent films from Asia, Africa and Latin America are screened in Bruges.

International Independent Film Festival, Brussels (www.centre multimedia.org) In early November, independent filmmakers from 60 countries screen more than 100 innovative films over a week.

Best
Gay & Lesbian

Brussels is Belgium's magnet for gay and lesbian visitors. The legendary event is the city's monthly La Démence (www.lademence.com), when bold and beautiful boys from all over Europe come to kick up their heels. The Festival du Film Gay & Lesbien de Bruxelles (www.fglb.org) takes place in late January, while the Belgian Gay & Lesbian Pride hits the streets in May. In general, the attitude to gay visitors is relaxed and accepting; in terms of legislation, Belgium is progressive about rights for same-sex couples.

AFP/GETTY IMAGES ©

The Scene

Brussels' gay and lesbian scene is concentrated around Rue du Marché au Charbon, Rue des Pierres and Rue de la Fourche in the heart of the city. Pick up the bimonthly booklet Zizo (in Dutch but easily navigable for nonspeakers), published by Holebifoon (www.holebifoon.be), which lists dozens of venues throughout the country. Bruges' one dedicated gay venue, **The Pub** (☎0477 26 07 40; www.r-en-k.be/atthepub; Hallestraat 4; ◷Mon & Thu-Sun 6pm-late), has been a long time coming: the tourist office keeps an updated list of other gay-friendly establishments.

Gay-friendly venues, Brussels

Le You Hosts a gay tea dance every Sunday. (p82)

Fontainas Hip and happening gay-friendly bar. (p80)

☑ **Top Tip**

After La Démence, many revellers kick on at the **Royal Windsor Hotel** (☎02-505 55 55; www.royalwindsorbrussels.com; Rue Duquesnoy 5).

Best
Markets

PASCALE BEROUJON/GETTY IMAGES©

The full spectrum of markets set up regularly in Bruges and Brussels – from elegant antiques markets and fairs trading rare china, crystal and furniture, through to flea markets spilling over with *brocante* (bric-a-brac) and secondhand treasures, including dog-eared comics, CDs and old vinyl records, plus new and vintage clothing. There are also rainbowlike food markets where you can pick up the ingredients for the perfect picnic.

Market Nosh

Any time of year, the street fare sold from caravans parked at the markets is a treat: try steaming waffles that tickle your nose with icing sugar and cones full of mayonnaise-slathered fries.

Christmas Markets

Christmas season brings the most magical markets of all, when the cities' ancient squares fill with stalls selling handcrafted toys, nutcrackers, a dazzling array of ornaments and warming mugs of sweet mulled wine. Winter wonderlands of ice sculptures and outdoor skating rinks are erected most years (both generally take place throughout the month of December). Tourist offices can advise the markets' venues, but you can't go wrong by just following the crowds.

Best Markets, Bruges

The Markt Historic Wednesday market ringed by stunning buildings. (p24)

Vismarkt The city's old fish market still purveys seafood and crafts. (p41)

Best Markets, Brussels

Gare du Midi Market Piled with North African and Mediterranean goodies. (p119)

Jeu-de-Balle fleamarket A favourite with local shoppers. (p119)

Sablon Antiques Market Mosey around for treasures at this weekend market. (p101)

Grand Place Hosts a flower market three times a week. (p68)

Place Jourdan Market Sunday market for food and clothes. (p115)

Best
Shops

Beer and chocolate top most shopping lists for visitors to Brussels and Bruges, and the cities have an astonishing array of both. Other unique suitcase-stuffers include handmade lace, designer fashions, classic comics, diamonds and quality antiques. Bargain hunters should visit during the two annual sales periods – the first week in January and the first week of July.

JONATHAN SMITH/GETTY IMAGES©

Buying Chocolate

Glinting light-brown, dark-brown and creamy-white coated squares, oblongs, balls and cups, embossed gold stamps and elaborate swirls, and wrapped in shimmering tinfoil or twisted inside cellophane. Yes, even shopping for chocolate is an art in Belgium – and it would want to be, with premium chocolates reaching €120 per kilo. A turning point for Belgian chocolate came in 1912, when pralines (filled chocolates) were created in Brussels. Today these are undergoing another evolution at the hands of Belgium's mould-breaking chocolatiers, whose fusion pralines incorporate flavours such as Havana cigar, cauliflower, green pea, chilli and wasabi.

Outlets

In addition to the rarefied showrooms of top chocolatiers there are also numerous luxury chains. Popular local manufacturers include Leonidas, the original praline creator, Neuhaus, and Galler, which also offers its superb pralines (such as fresh pistachio-filled white chocolate) in chocolate-bar form.

☑ **Top Tip**

You'll find many top chocolate brands in supermarkets for a fraction of the price you pay at the boutiques. Temptation prevails right up until leaving the country – Brussels International Airport is the biggest chocolate-selling point in the world.

Best for Chocolate, Brussels

Mary Long-established speciality praline maker. (p101)

Pierre Marcolini High-profile designer chocolates. (p101)

Neuhaus Brussel's original chocolatier in the Galerie de la Reine. (p84)

Galeries St-Hubert (p76)

Laurent Gerbaud Attractive handmade chocs in original flavours. (p96)

Best for Fine Food, Chocolate and Beer, Bruges

Bacchus Cornelius Sells a fantastic variety of beers and *jenevers*. (p29)

Diksmuids Boterhuis Picturesque grocer selling fine meats and cheeses. (p29)

2-Be Belgian specialities including chocolates, *jenever* and beers. (p43)

Chocolate Line Sells delicious handmade and experimental chocolates. (p62)

Best Fashion, Bruges

L'Heroine An oasis of designer cool in Bruges. (p29)

Madam Mim Second-hand garments plus some handmade with vintage fabrics. (p29)

Olivier Strelli Colourful and sophisticated fashion for men and women. (p43)

Best Covered Arcades, Brussels

Galeries St-Hubert Follow in the shopping footsteps of Victor Hugo. (p76)

Passage du Nord Pretty arcade with an oyster bar and chocolate shop. (p84)

Best Speciality Shops, Brussels

Boutique Tintin The best of Hergé's boy reporter. (p83)

De Biertempel Piled to the ceiling with speciality beers. (p84)

Best Speciality Shops, Bruges

't Apostelientje Wonderful handmade and vintage lace. (p31)

Rombaux Beautiful family-run music shop well worth a browse. (p42)

De Striep A wonderfully comprehensive stock of comic books. (p63)

Best
Museums & Galleries

Brussels and Bruges have a rich artistic tradition stretching back centuries; in true Belgian style, you'll also find irreverent sculptures and comic murals on display. The art movement that really captured Belgium's sense of the absurd was surrealism, and leading the charge was René Magritte, whose man in a bowler hat has become a national emblem.

Belgian Art

The distinction between Dutch and Flemish painters didn't come about until the late 16th century. However, the artists who were commissioned in the 15th century by nobility to record their life, times and religion, and would go on to influe=nce the direction of European art, are today known as the Flemish Primitives. The 16th century saw Flemish painter Pieter Brueghel the Elder and his two sons, Pieter the Younger and Jan, make their mark on the artistic landscape. Perhaps Belgium's most renowned painter, though, was Peter Paul Rubens (1577–1640). Born in Germany, Rubens returned to his parents' home town of Antwerp and utilised both Flemish and Italian styles to create his seminal religious works and voluptuous 'Rubenesque' nudes.

Contemporary Art

These days there's a powerful contemporary art scene in Belgium. Look out for works by Panamarenko, whose bizarre sculptures fuse authentic and imaginary flying contraptions; Jan Fabre, famed for his Bic-art (ballpoint drawings); powerful politically themed paintings by Luc Tuymans; and Eddy Stevens, who combines elements of Rubens' lustrous realism with surrealist twists.

ILPO MUSTO/ALAMY ©

Best for the Flemish Primitives

Musées Royaux des Beaux-Arts A wonderful Brussels showcase of the work of van der Weyden and co. (p88)

Groeningemuseum Bruges museum with sublime works by the masters of refined oil painting. (p46)

Memlingmuseum Six jewel-bright works by the great Hans Memling, in Bruges. (p48)

Best for Decorative Arts, Brussels

Musées Royaux des Beaux-Arts Art nouveau and art deco treasures. (p88)

Musée Horta Horta's own wonderfully designed home. (p116)

Fall of Icarus (1558) by Pieter Brueghel the Elder

Best Speciality Museums, Brussels

Musée du Costume et de la Dentelle Stunning lace-bedecked clothes. (p74)

Musée du Cacao et du Chocolat The history of Belgian chocolate. (p74)

Musée des Instruments de Musique Fascinating and unusual music museum. (p90)

Magritte Museum Surrealist fun: paintings, films, photos and sketches. (p89)

Best Speciality Museums, Bruges

Kantcentrum Quaint lace museum where you can see the stuff being crafted. (p31)

Museum voor Volkskunde An appealing folk museum in an old *godshuis*. (p30)

Choco-Story All you ever wanted to know about chocolate. (p34)

't Begijnhuisje Peek inside a typical old *begijnhof* home. (p51)

Frietmuseum Only in Belgium: a celebration of chips. (p35)

Diamantmuseum Lots of sparklers, and diamond-polishing demos. (p54)

Best
Parks & Gardens

The cities' parks and gardens offer more than a breath of fresh air; they're also oases of art, history and culture. The big smoke, Brussels, is greener than you might expect: the website www.ecli.net/rbc, in French and Dutch, lists every park in the Brussels Capital Region. Bruges has some beautiful parks lining its waterways, including one dotted with working windmills.

Brussels Parks

The most popular of Brussels' parks – attracting everyone from lunching office-workers to joggers and pram-pushing parents – is the Parc de Bruxelles. In the shadow of the Palais Royal and the Palais de la Nation, this gracious former hunting ground was laid out in the 18th century, and was the scene of bloody fighting in 1830 during Belgium's bid for independence. Near the EU, the vast Parc du Cinquantenaire is ringed by museums. At the city's southeastern edge, the wooded parkland of the Bois de la Cambre sprawls to meet the forest of the Forêt de Soignes; while in the city's northwest, the chestnut- and magnolia-shaded Parc de Laeken extends to the Atomium.

Best Green Spaces, Brussels

Parc du Cinquantenaire
Green space surrounded by top museums. (p104)

Parc Léopold Take a leafy break in the heart of the EU area. (p111)

Best Green Spaces, Bruges

Minnewater Secluded paths wind around Bruges' 'Lake of Love'. (p57)

Begijnhof The peaceful courtyard is dotted with daffodils in spring. (p50)

JEAN-BERNARD CARILLET/GETTY IMAGES©

Best **For Kids**

The exquisite chocolate boutiques and the comic museum might be aimed squarely at adults, but little visitors will still get a kick out of visiting these two cities. Travelling between the cities is a cinch; train journeys starting after 9am are free for kids under 12, accompanied by an adult.

JEAN-BERNARD CARILLET/GETTY IMAGES©

Kiddie Practicalities

Many B&Bs and hotels have baby cribs, but it's a good idea to reserve these as there is often only one available. Think twice about bringing a stroller, however, as you'll be wrestling it up and down endless flights of stairs and negotiating narrow footpaths and cobblestones. Dining with kids is rarely a problem, even at top-end establishments, but you'll never see Belgian children running amok, and you will be expected to make sure that yours aren't either. Restaurants often have high chairs, and sometimes special children's menus, but it's worth confirming in advance. With waffles and fries proliferating throughout both cities, you may be in for a bit of arm-twisting, but kids won't go hungry.

Best for a Rainy Day, Bruges

De Striep A comic-book cornucopia, great for kids. (p63)

Diamantmuseum Older children might enjoy the diamond-polishing sessions. (p54)

Best for a Rainy Day, Brussels

Centre Belge de la Bande Dessinée Temple to all things Tintin. (p70)

Théâtre Royal de Toone Fabulous and traditional puppet theatre. (p82)

Musée du Cacao et du Chocolat Chocolate making and tasting. (p74)

Scientastic Museum Subterranean science fun. (p75)

Best of the rest, Brussels

Manneken Pis Nothing will cheer up grumpy kids like the peeing boy. (p74)

Jeanneke Pis If that doesn't work, try his female counterpart. (p74)

Le Village de la Bande Dessinée Tuck in at this cartoon-bedecked cafe. (p99)

Mural-spotting Take the kids on a cartoon-mural themed walk (p74)

Musée des Sciences Naturelles Walk with the dinosaurs at this stunning museum. (p109)

Best
Architecture

Bruges and Brussels both present a compelling cross-section of architectural styles – indeed, the fabulous architecture is the reason many visitors are here. The country's most bizarre building, the Atomium, captures the futuristic style of the dawn of the space age. Contemporary architecture has lagged behind (evidenced by the nondescript glass office-blocks in the EU quarter of Brussels), but a few groundbreaking buildings are rising on the skyline, such as Bruges' red-brick concert hall, the Concertgebouw.

BERNAL REVERT/ALAMY©

Architectural History

Medieval architecture – the columned Romanesque and more angular Gothic – was followed in the 16th and early 17th centuries by Flemish baroque (also known as Flemish Renaissance), inspired by flamboyant trends from Italy. The most famous examples are the gorgeous guildhalls on Brussels' Grand Place, which were rebuilt in this style following the city's bombardment in 1695.

Art Nouveau and Beyond

The late 19th-century introduction of art nouveau has left a lasting mark, especially in Brussels. First introduced to the city by Victor Horta, signature art nouveau motifs of sinuous swirls, curls and floral tendrils are ubiquitous throughout Brussels, though the style would have left much more of a mark had it not been for the wave of demolitions that swept the city in the mid-20th century. The destruction of Horta's magnificent Maison du Peuple – torn down in 1965 to make way for an unutterably bland office building – sparked international outrage, leading to the introduction of laws protecting the city's heritage.

☑ **Top Tip**

Get up close and personal with Brussels' architecture with the resident-run heritage conservation group, **ARAU** (Atelier de Recherche et d'Action Urbaines; Map p72, D2; www.arau. org; Blvd Adolphe Max 55; ☾ Apr–mid-Dec), which runs excellent coach trips (€17) and walking tours (€10) taking you into buildings that are often otherwise off-limits. Book direct or through the tourist office.

Art nouveau Falstaff café, Brussels

Best Art Nouveau Buildings, Brussels

Musée Horta The master architect's sublime self-designed home. (p116)

Old England building Gorgeous old department store, now housing a music museum. (p91)

Centre Belge de la Bande Dessinée Housed in a gorgeous Horta building. (p70)

Falstaff Enjoy a beer in this bar designed by Houbion. (p81)

Maison Cauchie Art nouveau glamour in the EU district. (p105)

Best Churches, Brussels

Église Notre Dame du Sablon Medieval gem above a lovely square. (p94)

Cathédrale des Sts-Michel & Gudule Grand cathedral in the style of Paris' Notre Dame. (p94)

Église Notre-Dame de la Chapelle The oldest church in the capital. (p94)

Best Churches, Bruges

Jeruzalemkerk Dramatically modelled on the Church of the Holy Sepulchre in Jerusalem. (p31)

Onze-Lieve-Vrouwekerk Huge 13th-century church with a Michaelangelo statue. (p53)

St-Salvatorskathedraal Vast ancient church containing brasses and artworks. (p53)

Best of the Rest, Brussels

Grand Place Ringed by splendid gabled guild-houses. (p68)

Galeries St-Hubert Glamorous glassed-covered shopping arcade. (p76)

Palais de Justice Monumental and brooding law courts. (p95)

Berlaymont Building Star-shaped building housing EU commissioners. (p111)

Best of the Rest, Bruges

OLV-ter-Potterie Baroque church-hospital complex. (p34)

Concertgebouw Bruges' dramatic concession to modernity. (p61)

Best
Festivals &
Events

Not even the notoriously fickle climate can rain on Belgium's parade when it's time to party. Brussels and Bruges each host a slew of diverse events, especially midyear. And the short distances between the cities means you're only a train ride away from some sort of festivity. In addition to the tourist offices' websites, a good place to find out what's on is *Agenda* (www.brusselsagenda.be), a lively events magazine published weekly in English, French and Dutch. Many festival dates vary from year to year; check the websites for details.

Party All Night

One of the annual highlights in Brussels is the **Nuit Blanche** (www.brusselsinternational.be) in September. The idea is borrowed from Paris and has spread globally: for one 'white night', the capital stays up until sunrise, laying on a swath of events including projections, installations, circus acts and parties, blues and more in Brussels' Jardin Botanique.

Procession of the Holy Blood

A unique and ancient Bruges event is the **Heilig-Bloedprocessie** (www.holyblood.com) on Ascension Day, when a phial of what is said to be Christ's blood is paraded through the town accompanied by dance groups, floats and actors. It's by far the city's biggest and most important festival, with up to 3000 participants and 30–45,000 spectators every year.

Best Festivals for Music, Brussels

Ars Musica, Brussels (March; www.arsmusica.be) Audiences get wired into the contemporary music scene at this accessible festival.

Brussels Jazz Marathon, Brussels (May; www.brusselsjazzmarathon.be) Get bussed free to 125 gratis citywide concerts, featuring 400-plus artists over three jazz-fuelled days in late May.

Les Nuits Botanique, Brussels (May; www.lesnuits.be) Twelve days of rock, reggae, ska, hip-hop, electro, folk, rap, blues and more in Brussels' Jardin Botanique.

Couleur Café Festival, Brussels (June; www.couleurcafe.be) Performers at this three-day world music and dance knees-up in late June have included James Brown and UB40.

Musicians performing during the Brussels Jazz Marathon

Best Festivals for Music, Bruges

Musica Antiqua, Bruges (August; www.festival. be) This festival of early music not only includes concerts but also hands-on workshops such as harpsichord maintenance.

Klinkers, Bruges (August; www.klinkers -brugge.be) Eleven-day music fest culminating in Benewerk (legwork), featuring dancing from salsa to folk to '80s.

Best Festivals for Food and Drink, Brussels

Choco-Laté, Bruges (April; www.choco-late. be) Some years see a small chocolate market, others a full-blown festival with everything from tastings to chocolate beauty-treatments, chocolate-and-wine pairing and a 'kids village'.

Belgian Beer Weekend, Brussels (September; www.weekenddelabiere. be) The Grand Place is overtaken by a veritable village of stalls selling beer and associated paraphernalia (glasses, coasters etc). Drink prices are reasonable and entry is free.

Best of the Rest, Brussels

Dring Dring Bike Festival, Brussels (May; www. dringdring.be) Buy new and secondhand bikes, learn to navigate city traffic, and take guided trips or – if you missed out as a kid – adult cycling lessons.

Ommegang, Brussels (July; www.ommegang. be) Dating from the 14th century, this medieval-style procession kicks off from the Place du Grand Sablon, ending with a dance on the illuminated Grand Place.

Brussels Summer Festival, Brussels (August; www.infofestival.be) Free 10-day bash packing in more than 140 different performances (concerts, children's theatre and more), including lots of local acts.

Comics Festival, Brussels (October; www. comicsfestivalbelgium. com) Rub shoulders with the artists and writers behind some of Belgium's best-known comic characters.

Best
Tours

Best Bus & Boat Tours

Brussels by Water

(☎02-203 64 06; www.scaldisnet.be; Ave du Port; 45min port tours adult/concession from €4/3; ☺2pm, 3pm, 4pm & 5pm Tue, Wed & Sun May-Sep) A unique and unexpected way to see Brussels is from the water. Various educational tours explore the canal that cuts through the city, and there are also cruise options with live music and a drink thrown in.

Brussels City Tours

(☎02-513 77 44; www.brussels-city-tours.com; Rue de la Colline 8; adult/concession/child €26/23/13; ☺every 30min, 10am-3pm) The Grand City Tour covers everything from the Atomium to the EU, and includes some lovely art nouveau houses. You kick off with a walking tour of the Grand Place, and are then transported by coach.

Best Bicycle Tours

Brussels Bike Tours

(☎0484 89 89 36; www.brusselsbiketours.com; tour inc bicycle rental adult/student €22/25; ☺10am Feb-Nov, 10am & 3pm Apr-Sep) These four-hour tours (maximum group size 12) start from the Hôtel de Ville (Grand Place). Many first-time visitors love both the ride and the beer and *frites* stops along the way (food and drink cost extra).

Quasimundo Bike Tours

(☎050 33 07 75; www.quasimundo.com; tour incl bicycle rental adult/student €25/23; ☺10am Mar-Oct) Explore Bruges by bike on a classic 2.5-hour trip taking in narrow backstreets, the medieval walls, windmills and – of course – the canals. The four-hour 'Border by Bike' tour takes you as far as the Dutch border, via Damme, Oostkerke castle and assorted canals and windmills.

Best Specialist Tours

Horse-drawn Carriage Tours

(Markt, Bruges; 30min tour €39 per carriage; ☺9am-early eve, depending on demand) Touristy and

PASCALE BEROUJON/GETTY IMAGES ©

☑ **Top Tip**

Pick up USE-IT's free leaflet for self-guided walking tours off the beaten track in Brussels.

cheesy it might be, but you'll learn a lot about Bruges from the carriage tours, and there's an undeniable charm to exploring the cobbled lanes and canals the old-fashioned way.

USE-IT Tours

(☎02-725 52 75; www.use-it.be; Steenkoolkaai 9B, Brussels; ☺10am-1pm & 2-6pm Mon-Sat) Offers free informal tours of different Brussels neighbourhoods, focusing on street life and society rather than history, depart from the office in Ste-Catherine.

Survival Guide

Survival Guide

Before You Go

When to Go

°C/°F Temp   **Rainfall** inches/mm
30/86—   — 4/100
20/68—
10/50—   — 2/5
0/32—
-10/14—   — 0
        J F M A M J J A S O N D

➡ **Winter (Nov-Feb)**
Short, cold days with occasional snow. Museums and attractions are quieter, and prices are generally lower. A good time to visit Bruges.

➡ **Spring (Mar-May)**
Cold to mild; often wet and blustery. Major sights start getting busier; parks and gardens begin to blossom.

➡ **Summer (Jun-Aug)**
Weather mainly sunny, though it may rain at times. Main tourist season. A great time for music festivals.

➡ **Autumn (Sep-Nov)**
Mild, mixed weather. Good for exhibitions and the arts.

Book Your Stay

➡ Brussels abounds with accommodation options, including over 14,000 hotel rooms. Most are geared for midweek Eurocrats, which means there are often astounding deals for tourists, especially on weekends.

➡ Top-end hotels often charge extra for breakfast on weekdays, but throw in lavish weekend buffets.

➡ Some midrange and top-end establishments also slash their rates during the summer holidays (roughly mid-July to mid-September).

➡ Bruges is the exact opposite of Brussels: hotels are packed and prices tend to be higher on weekends. Book well ahead for high season (approximately Easter to late October) and for December's Christmas markets.

Useful Websites

Lonely Planet (www.lonely planet.com/hotels) Author-penned reviews of Lonely Planet's top choices.

Bed & Brussels (www.bnb -brussels.be) Many B&Bs in Bruges and Brussels can be booked through Bed & Brussels, which also offers various packages.

VisitBrussels (visit brussels.be) Reservations can be made for free via the Brussels tourist office website.

Hostelling International (www.hihostels.com) For booking HI hostels.

Best Budget

Lybeer Travellers' Hostel, Bruges (www. hostellybeer.com) Homey hostel in the process of being regenerated.

Bauhaus, Bruges (www. bauhaus.be) The city's backpacker village, a self-proclaimed legend.

2go4, Brussels (www.2go4.be) Bargain dorms and doubles in the heart of town.

Bruegel, Brussels (www. hihostels.com/dba/ hostels-Brussels--- Bruegel-008007.en.htm)

Good location near the Grand Place.

Van Gogh Hostel, Brussels (www.chab.be) One of the best equipped hostels in town.

Best Midrange

B&B Huyze Hertsberge, Bruges (www.huyze hertsberge.be) Soothing pale colours and a great canal-side location.

Bourgoensch Hof, Bruges (www.hotel -bourgoensch-hof.be) Amazingly affordable rooms in the heart of Bruges.

Chambres en Ville, Brussels (www.chambresen ville.be) Fantastically elegant rooms and studios.

B&B Phileas Fogg, Brussels (www.phileasfogg.be) Glamorous décor and a global theme.

Best Top-End

Relais Ravestein, Bruges (www.relaisravestein.be) Grand and palatial suites.

Guesthouse Nuit Blanche, Bruges (www. bruges-bb.com/bed-and -breakfast.htm) Utterly romantic 15th-century house filled with antiques.

Hôtel Métropole, Brussels (www.metropole hotel.com) Marbled opulence around every corner.

The White Hotel, Brussels (www.thewhitehotel. be) As the name suggests, everything is white; very easy on the eye.

Monty Small Design Hotel, Brussels (www. monty-hotel.be) Funky décor and creature comforts.

Arriving in Bruges & Brussels

☑ **Top Tip** For the best way to get to your accommodation, see p17.

Brussels Airport

Brussels International Airport (www.brussels airport.be) is 14km northeast of the city; the arrivals hall (Level 2) has a money changer (but watch the rates), car-rental agencies and tourist information. The bus terminus and luggage lockers are on Level 0; the train station is on Level 1.

➡ **Brussels Airport Express** runs four times an hour from 5.26am with the last train leaving at 12.26am (5.17am and 11.50pm respectively on weekends) to Brussels' Gare du Nord (18 minutes), Gare Centrale (22 minutes) and Gare du Midi (30 minutes). The trip costs €4.40/2.90 one way (1st/2nd class).

➡ **MIVB/STIB** (www.stib. be) runs express buses (line 12 on weekdays, line 11 on weekends) from the airport to Schuman metro station and then on to Gare Bruxelles-Luxembourg. The service runs regularly from 7am to 8pm (outside these hours and on weekends Schuman is the last stop) taking roughly 30 minutes. Tickets cost €3.

➡ **DeLijn** (www.delijn. be) also runs a bus (€3) between the airport and Gare du Nord, but the Brussels Airport Express is much faster.

➡ A taxi to central Brussels will cost around €35.

Brussels South Charleroi Airport

Brussels' second airport, Brussels South Charleroi Airport (www.charleroi -airport.com), is 46km southeast of the city and is used mainly by budget airlines, including Ryanair.

➡ Buses to Brussels Gare du Midi leave around half an hour after flight arrivals (€11/20 one way/ return; one hour).

➡ There are also direct buses to Bruges four times per day (€20/38 one way/ return; two hours).

Brussels Gare du Midi

➡ The **Eurostar** (www. eurostar.com) whisks you between Brussels' Gare du Midi and central London's St Pancras In-

---

Transport Tours in Brussels

➡ **Brussels by Water** (☎02-203 64 06; www.scaldisnet.be; Ave du Port; 45-min port tours adult/concession from €4/3; ☻2pm, 3pm, 4pm & 5pm Tue, Wed & Sun May-Sep) Brussels' canals offer an interesting (if industrial) perspective on the capital.

➡ **Pro Velo** (☎02-502 73 55; www.provelo.org; Rue de Londres 15; tours from €8) Arranges good self-guided bicycle tours.

Transport Tours in Bruges

➡ **Canal cruises** Several companies run from docks on the Dijver, Rozenhoedkaai and by the Blinde Ezelstraat bridge, departing every 20 minutes in summer.

➡ **Horse-drawn carriage tours** (€39 per carriage for a 30-min tour.) Touristy but historically informative tours set off from the Markt.

➡ **Quasimundo bike tours** (☎050 33 07 75; www.quasimundo.com; tour incl bicycle rental adult/student €25/23; ☻10am Mar-Oct) Guided cycling tour exploring Bruges' back streets.

ternational Station in just one hour, 51 minutes.

➡ There are two trains an hour from Brussels to Bruges (from €18 one way; 50 minutes).

Bruges Railway Station

➡ Bruges' train station is 1.5km south of Markt

➡ There are regular buses into town, or you'll easily find a taxi.

➡ Twice-hourly trains run to Brussels via Ghent. Hourly trains go to Antwerp, Knokke, Ostend and Zeebrugge via Lissewege.

Getting Around

Bicycle
☑ **Best for**... making like a local

➡ **Villo!** (☑ 07-805 11 10; http://en.villo.be; ☼ 24hr) is a system of 180 automated stations for short-term bicycle rental in Brussels. First you need a subscription, then charges accumulate and

are debited from your credit/bank card.

➡ In Brussels, bicycles can be carried on metros and trams except at rush hours (7am to 9am and 4pm to 6.30pm), once you've purchased a one-year bike pass (€15).

➡ **Cycling In Brussels** (www.bicycle.irisnet.be) has maps and information.

➡ Bruges is a great city for cyclists – it won't take you long to get anywhere, even to the coast, by bike.

➡ For bike rental in Bruges, including tandems, try **Eric Popelier** (☑ 050 34 32 62; www.fietsenpopelier.be; Mariastraat 26; per hr/half-/full day €4/8/12, tandem per hr/half-/full day €10/17/25; ☼ 10am-6pm).

Boat
☑ **Best for**... Bruges romantics

➡ Boats depart roughly every 20 minutes from the jetties south of the Burg, including Rozenhoedkaai and Dijver.

➡ Tours last around 30 minutes (adult/child €7.60/3.40)

➡ Expect queues in summer.

Car & Motorcycle
☑ **Best for**... independence

➡ Public transport is the easiest way to get round Brussels: the slightest hiccup brings traffic to a halt, especially on Friday afternoons.

➡ In Brussels, street parking requires payment when signs say *betalend parkeren/stationnement payant* (usually 9am to 1pm and 2pm to 7pm Monday to Saturday).

➡ Major car-rental companies have offices at Gare du Midi and Brussels Airport, but rentals from their downtown offices usually cost less. Try **Avis** (☑ 02-537 12 80; www.avis.be; Rue Américaine 145) or **Budget** (☑ 02-646 51 30; www.budget.be; Ave Louise 91).

Given central Bruges' nightmarish one-way system, the best idea for drivers is to use the large covered car park beside the train station, which is reasonably priced.

Metro, Premetro & Bus
☑ **Best for**... outlying areas in Brussels

➡ Brussels' vast web of bus and tram transport

Tickets & Passes

In Brussels, transport tickets are valid for one hour and are sold at metro stations, STIB/MIVB kiosks, newsagents and on buses and trams. Single STIB/MIVB tickets cost €1.80 including transfers, while unlimited one-day passes cost €6. Note that airport buses are excluded and slightly higher 'jump' fares apply if you want to connect to city routes operated by De Lijn (Flanders bus), TEC (Wallonia bus) or SNCB/NMBS (rail). Children under six travel free. Tickets must be validated before travel, in machines located at the entrance to metro platforms or inside buses and trams. Travelling with an unvalidated ticket will incur a fine; random checks are made.

has no central hub, so grab a free STIB/MIVB transport map before going too far.

➡ Underground premetro trams link Brussels-Nord (Gare du Nord) and Brussels-Midi (Gare du Midi) via the Bourse.

➡ Don't expect London-style frequency: trains only run every 10 to 15 minutes.

➡ Public transport in Brussels runs from 6am to midnight, after which it's taxi only except on Friday and Saturday, when 17 Noctis night-bus routes (€3 one way) operate twice hourly from midnight to 3am, most starting from Place de Brouckère.

Taxi

☑ **Best for**... late nights

➡ Official taxis (typically black or white) charge

€2.40 pick-up plus €1.35/2.70 per kilometre within/outside Brussels. There's a €2 supplement between 10pm and 6am. Waiting costs €25 per hour.

➡ Taxes and tips are officially included in the meter price so you should ignore requests for extra service charges.

➡ Taxis in Brussels wait near the three central train stations, outside Hôtel Amigo, near the Grand Place and at Place Stéphanie on Ave Louise.

➡ Cabbies have a reputation for aggressive, over-fast driving but if you're seriously dissatisfied you can report them toll-free on 0800 940 01 – the receipt, which they must legally print for you, should have their four-digit taxi ID.

➡ In Brussels, try **Taxis Bleus** (☎02-268 00 00) or **Taxis Verts** (☎02-349 49 49).

➡ In Bruges, taxis wait on the Markt and in front of the train station. Otherwise you can phone 050 33 44 44 or 050 38 46 60.

Essential Information

Business Hours

Reviews in this book won't list business hours unless they vary significantly from these standards.

➡ **Restaurants** 11.30am to 3pm & 6.30pm to 11pm

➡ **Brasseries** 11am to 1am

➡ **Cafés** 10am to 5am; closing times usually depend on how busy a place is on any given night

➡ **Banks** 9am to 3.30pm

➡ **Shops** 9am to 6pm Monday to Saturday; some also open on Sunday

☑ **Top Tip** Post offices generally operate from 9am to 5pm Monday to Friday and until noon Saturday. Smaller branches close for lunch; larger ones stay open until 6pm.

Discount Cards

☑ **Top Tip** If you're planning on some serious sightseeing, you'll save a bundle with the Brussels Card or Bruges Card – they also give discounts at some concert venues, restaurants and bars, as well as saving you money on transport.

➡ Many of Belgium's attractions and entertainment venues offer discounts for students and children; family rates are rare.

➡ Students will need an International Student Identity Card (ISIC) for reduced admission to museums, discounted cinema tickets and train fares. Senior citizens and travellers with disabilities will generally receive a discount.

Electricity

230V/50Hz

Emergency

➡ **Ambulance/Fire Brigade** (☎100)

➡ **Police** (☎101)

➡ **Helpline** (☎02-648 40 14) A 24-hour helpline based in Brussels.

➡ **SOS Viol** (☎02-534 36 36) Rape crisis line in Brussels.

Money

➡ **Currency** Belgium uses the euro (€). For updated currency exchange rates, check www.xe.com.

➡ **ATMs** Widely available in Brussels and Bruges.

➡ **Credit cards** Visa is the most widely accepted credit card, followed by MasterCard. American Express and Diners Club cards are only accepted at the more exclusive establishments.

➡ **Money changers** There are exchange bureaus (*wisselkantoren* in Dutch, *bureaux d'échange* in French) at airports or train stations as well as major tourist precincts. Few establishments accept travellers' cheques.

➡ **Tipping** Tipping is not obligatory, as service and VAT are included in hotel and restaurant prices. It's common to round up restaurant bills and taxi fares by a euro or two. In public toilets people are expected to tip the attendants (€0.30 to €0.50).

Public Holidays

New Year's Day
1 January

Easter Monday
March/April

Labour Day 1 May

Ascension Day
40th day after Easter

Whit Monday 7th Monday after Easter

Money-Saving Tips

➡ Both cities offer useful discount cards for museums, transport and eating and entertainment discounts (see www.bruggecitycard.be for Bruges, or www.brusselscard.be for Brussels).

➡ On the first Wednesday of the month, many Brussels museums are free from 1pm.

➡ The Arsène office at the tourist office in Brussels offers heavily discounted tickets for cultural events (Rue Royale 2; ⏱noon-5pm Tue-Sat).

➡ Food markets in both cities offer great supplies for self-caterers at reasonable prices.

Festival of the Flemish Community
11 July

Belgium National Day
21 July

Assumption Day
15 August

All Saints' Day
1 November

Armistice Day
11 November

Christmas Day
25 December

Safe Travel

While the rate of violent crime in Belgium is low compared with many European countries, petty theft does occur, more so in larger cities. Pickpocket haunts in Brussels include the Grand Place, the narrow streets around Ilôt Sacré, Rue Neuve, and the markets at Gare du Midi and Place du Jeu-de-Balle.

Telephone

Mobile Phones
Belgium uses the GSM 900/1800 cellular system, compatible with phones from the UK, Australia and most of Asia (and all tri-band phones), but not GSM 1900 phones from North America or the separate Japanese system.

Phone Codes
Belgium's international country code is 32. Area codes for each city are incorporated into telephone numbers. You must dial the area code, even when dialling from within the relevant area. Telephone numbers given in this book include the necessary area codes.

Making International and Domestic Calls
➡ Public telephones that accept stored-value phonecards (available from post offices, telephone centres, newsstands and retail outlets) are the norm.

➡ You can use Skype to call internationally at internet cafes, and at the computer terminals of some hostels.

Useful Numbers

➡ **Directory assistance (English-speaking operator)** (☎1405)

➡ **International dialling code** (☎00)

➡ **International operator** (☎1324)

Toilets

Public toilets are generally clean and well looked after. You'll be given a foul look or reprimanded if you attempt to leave without tipping the attendant (€0.30 to €0.50); this goes for both men and women.

Tourist Information

Brussels

➡ **Visit Brussels** (☎02 513 89 40; http://visitbrussels.be; rue Royale 2; ☯9am-6pm Mon-Fri, 10am-6pm Sat-Sun) has stacks of excellent Brussels-specific information; there is another branch at the **Grand Place**.

➡ **Use-It** (☎02-725 52 75; www.use-it.be; Steenkoolkaai 9B; ☯10am-1pm & 2-6pm Mon-Sat) Friendly youth-oriented tourist office; they also do free alternative city tours.

Bruges

➡ Bruges' tourist office, **In & Uit Brugge** (☎050 44 46 46; www.brugge.be; 't Zand 34; ☯10am-6pm Mon-Sun) is located inside the contemporary, red-brick Concertgebouw.

➡ There is also a smaller branch (☯10am-5pm Mon-Fri, till 2pm Sat-Sun) located inside the train station.

☑ **Top Tip** The superb free USE-IT guide-maps are full of spot-on local tips and irreverent humour.

Travellers with Disabilities

Belgium's centuries-old buildings pose the biggest difficulty for travellers with mobility problems. Some public buildings, have lifts and/or ramps, but the majority don't. A 2000 law obliges architects to ensure buildings, including hotels and shops, are built in a 'disabled-friendly' way, but this will take time.

Outdoors, wheelchair users are up against uneven cobblestones, narrow pavements and steep kerbs. When travelling on trains, wheelchair users must give an hour's notice. The website for Belgian Railways has detailed information for mo-

bility-impaired passengers (www.b-rail.be/nat/E/practical/limitedmobility). Alternatively, contact their customer service department. Only a handful of Brussels' metro stations have lifts (elevators), but this number is gradually increasing. Likewise, Brussels' new leather-seated trams, which are currently being rolled out, are wheelchair accessible.

☑ **Top Tip** In Brussels, **Taxi Hendriks** (☎02-752 9800; www.hendriks.be in French & Dutch) has taxis that can accommodate wheelchairs.

Visas

➡ There are no entry requirements or restrictions on EU nationals visiting Belgium.

➡ Citizens of Australia, Canada, Israel, Japan, New Zealand and the USA do not need visas to visit the country as tourists for up to three months.

➡ Except for nationals from a few other European countries (such as Norway), everyone else must have a visa – check with Belgium's Ministry of Foreign Affairs (www.diplomatie.be) for info.

Dos & Don'ts

➡ Brussels is bilingual, but in Bruges you should speak English rather than French (see p158).

➡ When meeting for the first time, men and women, and women and women, greet each other with three kisses on the cheek (starting on the left): after that it's usually just one kiss (on the left). Men meeting men generally shake hands.

Language

Belgium's population is split between Dutch-speaking Flanders (*Vlaanderen* in Dutch) in the north and French-speaking Wallonia (*la Wallonie* in French) in the south, as well as a small German-speaking region in the east.

If you spend any time travelling around Belgium, you'll have to get used to switching between Dutch (*Nederlands*) and French (*français*). Bruges in the north is Flemish and therefore Dutch-speaking. Brussels is officially bilingual, though French has long been the city's dominant language.

Most of the sounds used when speaking both French and Dutch can be found in English. If you read our pronunciation guides below as if they were English, you'll be understood just fine.

To enhance your trip with a phrasebook, visit **lonelyplanet.com**. Lonely Planet iPhone phrasebooks are available through the Apple App store.

French – Basics

Hello.
Bonjour. — bon·zhoor

Goodbye.
Au revoir. — o·rer·vwa

How are you?
Comment allez-vous? — ko·mon ta·lay·voo

I'm fine, thanks.
Bien, merci. — byun mair·see

Please.
S'il vous plaît. — seel voo play

Thank you.
Merci. — mair·see

Excuse me.
Excusez-moi. — ek·skew·zay·mwa

Sorry.
Pardon. — par·don

Yes./No.
Oui./Non. — wee/non

Do you speak English?
Parlez-vous anglais? — par·lay·voo ong·glay

I don't understand.
Je ne comprends pas. — zher ner kom·pron pa

French – Eating & Drinking

A coffee, please.
Un café, s'il vous plaît — ewn ka·fay seel voo play

I'm a vegetarian.
Je suis végétarien/ végétarienne. (m/f) — zher swee vay·zhay·ta·ryun/ vay·zhay·ta·ryen

Cheers!
Santé! — son·tay

That was delicious.
C'était délicieux! — say·tay day·lee·syer

Please bring the bill.
L'addition, s'il vous plaît. — la·dee·syon seel voo play

French – Shopping

I'd like to buy ...
Je voudrais acheter ... — zher voo·dray ash·tay ...

I'm just looking.
Je regarde. — zher rer·gard

How much is it?
C'est combien? — say kom·byun

It's too expensive.
C'est trop cher. say tro shair

Can you lower the price?
Vous pouvez voo poo·vay
baisser le prix? bay·say ler pree

French – Emergencies

Help!
Au secours! o skoor

Call the police!
Appelez la police! a·play la po·lees

Call a doctor!
Appelez un a·play un
médecin! mayd·sun

I'm sick.
Je suis malade. zher swee ma·lad

I'm lost.
Je suis perdu/ zhe swee·pair·dew
perdue. (m/f)

Where are the toilets?
Où sont les oo son lay
toilettes? twa·let

French – Time & Numbers

What time is it?
Quelle heure kel er
est-il? ay til

It's (eight) o'clock.
Il est (huit) il ay (weet)
heures. er

It's half past (10).
Il est (dix) heures il ay (deez) er
et demie. ay day·mee

morning	*matin*	ma·tun
afternoon	*après-midi*	a·pray·mee·dee
evening	*soir*	swar
yesterday	*hier*	yair
today	*aujourd'hui*	o·zhoor·dwee
tomorrow	*demain*	der·mun

Monday	*lundi*	lun·dee
Tuesday	*mardi*	mar·dee
Wednesday	*mercredi*	mair·krer·dee
Thursday	*jeudi*	zher·dee
Friday	*vendredi*	von·drer·dee
Saturday	*samedi*	sam·dee
Sunday	*dimanche*	dee·monsh

1	*un*	un
2	*deux*	der
3	*trois*	trwa
4	*quatre*	ka·trer
5	*cinq*	sungk
6	*six*	sees
7	*sept*	set
8	*huit*	weet
9	*neuf*	nerf
10	*dix*	dees
100	*cent*	son
1000	*mille*	meel

French – Transport & Directions

Where's ...?
Où est ...? oo ay ...

What's the address?
Quelle est l'adresse? kel ay la·dres

Can you show me (on the map)?
Pouvez-vous poo·vay·voo
m'indiquer mun·dee·kay
(sur la carte)? (sewr la kart)

I want to go to ...
Je voudrais zher voo·dray
aller à ... a·lay a ...

What time does it leave?
À quelle heure a kel er
est-ce qu'il part? es kil par

Dutch – Basics

Hello.
Dag./Hallo.   dakh/ha·*loh*

Goodbye.
Dag.   dakh

How are you?
Hoe gaat het   hoo khaat huht
met u?   met ew

Fine. And you?
Goed. En met u?   khoot en met ew

Please.
Alstublieft.   al·stew·*bleeft*

Thank you.
Dank u.   dangk ew

Excuse me.
Excuseer mij.   eks·kew·*zeyr* mey

Yes./No.
Ja./Nee.   yaa/ney

Do you speak English?
Spreekt u Engels?   spreykt ew *eng*·uhls

I don't understand.
Ik begrijp het   ik buh·*khreyp* huht
niet.   neet

Dutch – Eating & Drinking

I'd like the menu, please.
Ik wil graag   ik wil khraakh
een menu.   uhn me·*new*

What would you recommend?
Wat kan u   wat kan ew
aanbevelen?   *aan*·buh·vey·luhn

Delicious!
Heerlijk!/Lekker!   heyr·luhk/le·kuhr

Cheers!
Proost!   prohst

Can I have the bill, please?
Mag ik de   makh ik duh
rekening   *rey*·kuh·ning
alstublieft?   al·stew·*bleeft*

breakfast	*ontbijt*	ont·*beyt*
lunch	*middagmaal*	mi·dakh·maal
dinner	*avondmaal*	aa·vont·maal

beer	*bier*	beer
bread	*brood*	broht
coffee	*koffie*	ko·fee
fish	*vis*	vis
meat	*vlees*	vleys
nuts	*noten*	noh·tuhn
red wine	*rode wijn*	roh·duh weyn
tea	*thee*	tey

Dutch – Shopping

I'd like to buy ...
Ik wil graag ...   ik wil khraakh ...
kopen.   koh·puhn

I'm just looking.
Ik kijk alleen maar.   ik keyk a·leyn maar

How much is it?
Hoeveel kost het?   hoo·*veyl* kost huht

That's too expensive.
Dat is te duur.   dat is tuh dewr

Can you lower the price?
Kunt u wat van de   kunt ew wat van duh
prijs afdoen?   preys *af*·doon

Do you have any others?
Heeft u nog   heyft ew nokh
andere?   *an*·duh·ruh

Dutch – Emergencies

Help!
Help!   help

Leave me alone!
Laat me met rust!   laat muh met rust

Call the police!
Bel de politie!   bel duh poh·*lee*·see

Call a doctor!
Bel een dokter!   bel uhn *dok*·tuhr

I'm sick.
Ik ben ziek.   ik ben zeek

I'm lost.
Ik ben verdwaald.   ik ben vuhr·*dwaalt*

Where are the toilets?
Waar zijn de   waar zeyn duh
toiletten?   twa·*le*·tuhn

Dutch – Time & Numbers
What time is it?
Hoe laat is het?   hoo laat is huht

It's (10) o'clock.
Het is (tien) uur.   huht is (teen) ewr

Half past (10).
Half (elf).   half (elf)
(lit: half eleven)

morning	*'s ochtends*	*sokh*·tuhns
afternoon	*'s middags*	*smi*·dakhs
evening	*'s avonds*	*saa*·vonts
yesterday	*gisteren*	*khis*·tuh·ruhn
today	*vandaag*	van·*daakh*
tomorrow	*morgen*	*mor*·khuhn

Monday	*maandag*	*maan*·dakh
Tuesday	*dinsdag*	*dins*·dakh
Wednesday	*woensdag*	*woons*·dakh
Thursday	*donderdag*	*don*·duhr·dakh
Friday	*vrijdag*	*vrey*·dakh
Saturday	*zaterdag*	*zaa*·tuhr·dakh
Sunday	*zondag*	*zon*·dakh

1	*één*	eyn
2	*twee*	twey
3	*drie*	dree
4	*vier*	veer
5	*vijf*	veyf
6	*zes*	zes
7	*zeven*	*zey*·vuhn
8	*acht*	akht
9	*negen*	*ney*·khuhn
10	*tien*	teen
100	*honderd*	*hon*·duhrt
1000	*duizend*	*döy*·zuhnt

Dutch – Transport & Directions
Where's ...?
Waar is ...?   waar is ...

What's the address?
Wat is het adres?   wat is huht a·*dres*

Can you show me (on the map)?
Kunt u het   kunt ew huht
mij tonen   mey *toh*·nuhn
(op de kaart)?   (op duh kaart)

Please take me to ...
Breng me   breng muh
alstublieft naar ...   al·stew·*bleeft* naar ...

What time does it leave?
Hoe laat   hoo laat
vertrekt het?   vuhr·*trekt* huht

A ticket to ..., please.
Een kaartje naar   uhn *kaar*·chuh naar
... graag.   ... khraakh

I'd like to hire a bicycle.
Ik wil graag   ik wil khraakh
een fiets huren.   uhn feets *hew*·ruhn

Index

See also separate subindexes for:

🗙 **Eating p173**

🍷 **Drinking p173**

☆ **Entertainment p173**

🔒 **Shopping p174**

Sights p000
Map Pages **p000**

Sights p000
Map Pages **p000**